THE AUTHOR

GERALD H. SLUSSER is a graduate of
Southern Methodist University and Austin Presbyterian Theological Seminary,
and he holds a doctorate from the University of Texas. He was Research Fellow at the University of Glasgow. As
pastor, he served two charges in Dallas,
Texas. At present he is Assistant Professor of Christian Education at Hartford
Seminary Foundation, School of Religious Education.

THE LOCAL CHURCH
IN
TRANSITION

THE LOCAL CHURCH
IN
TRANSITION

Theology, Education, and Ministry

by

GERALD H. SLUSSER

THE WESTMINSTER PRESS
Philadelphia

LIBRARY OF CONGRESS CATALOG CARD No. 64-16351

PUBLISHED BY THE WESTMINSTER PRESS ®

PHILADELPHIA, PENNSYLVANIA 19107

PRINTED IN THE UNITED STATES OF AMERICA

For
Peter and Andrew

Contents

THOUGH the theological task is never done and must constantly be undertaken *ab ovo,* none of us approaches the task alone, but each stands in the midst of a vast company whose presence is a constant inspiration—those who have gone before and those who will come after. Each of us begins his theological work with an inestimable debt to the past and an incalculable responsibility to the future, both of which drive him to do nothing more than try to learn from those who have preceded him so as to be able to pass on to those who shall follow the precious heritage that all must ever seek more adequately to express.

—SCHUBERT M. OGDEN, *Christ Without Myth,* p. 7.

Whether or not we are willing to accept the situation in our world today, the old has passed completely away, and we are, as always, being called by God to the new life in the land he has promised if we but trust him and not ourselves. The spirit of truth seeks that we should all know the truth. God is the spirit of truth and has sifted the world, judging it in its failure to meet and accept the truth as life-giving. If we will prove that we are his own, we will hear his voice and follow him, gathering together all others who will follow also. His word, as it came through Jesus Christ, will never leave us in peace until we have turned our back on Egypt and set our faces toward the wilderness of the future—the exodus—life's third act.

—DOROTHY M. SLUSSER,
At the Foot of the Mountain, p. 153.

Preface

THE PURPOSE of this book is to make a contribution to the contemporary discussion about the nature of the church and its ministry, particularly trying to relate theology to the practice of Christian education. On many sides today questions are being raised about the nature of Christian education; some persons even doubt that it has any place in the work of the church and especially doubt its value in the seminary curriculum. It is hoped that this book will answer some of these doubts and criticisms. It does so, however, not by defending any past pattern of theology, or Christian education, or ministry, but by trying in a constructive way to examine the place of all three of these and their interrelationship. Undertaking such a task is ambitious, to say the least, and could not have been accomplished without the incredible amount of work that has been done during the past decade to reevaluate the theological endeavor and the church. In this task I have tried to take seriously the heritage of the church as well as contemporary man and his future. To be serious means to dare to be critical, even of those from whom one has learned much. Thus, in the work there are many and serious criticisms stated and implied of some Christian educators and theologians whose work has been of great value to me both professionally and personally.

I am indebted to a host of teachers and friends, past and present, without whom this book would have been impossible. They must, however, remain unnamed, except as credit is given in the text and notes. Many of the ideas herein expressed have been formulated and used in lectures given in my courses at the Hartford Seminary Foundation, and I wish here to thank the many students who have taken the time to share with me their honest responses. Particularly, I must thank my wife, who has served as a very effective theological colleague and critic for me. She has also been invaluable in the preparation of the final manuscript. For their cheerful concern and willingness to work with some awkward manuscripts, I thank both my wife and Miss Ann LaBrecque, who were my typists.

G.H.S.

Hartford, Connecticut

Introduction

The Need for a New Image for
the Local Church and Its Ministry

ALMOST no one doubts any longer that, despite the numerical growth, there are some profound troubles with the American churches. There are, likewise, serious troubles in the churches of Europe and, though they are slightly different, their basic situation is quite similar. Sociological descriptions of the symptoms are not lacking,[1] but in each case such descriptions assume not only the validity of sociological analysis for the church but usually the author's theological position as well. Hence, though the descriptions are valuable and should stir concerned Christians, they do not point any viable way forward. More helpful are two recent books that suggest that the real problem lies with the working theology of the church, its own understanding of its message, and its relation to the world. Obviously, this kind of critique has been made before, but not since the early writing of Karl Barth has the case been made so clearly that the enemy within the church is even more important and more insidious than the enemy without.

A NEW ROLE FOR THE MINISTER

Daniel Jenkins, a well-known British theologian, is disturbed because the Protestant Church " frequently becomes a distraction rather than a source of help to Christian men concerned to ' overcome the world.' "[2] He suggests that the problem is too much religion, too little faith, and lack of wisdom to know the difference. He is convinced, nonetheless, that the church is vital and that there is a viable way forward. His way forward stresses two lines of action. First, "nothing must be allowed to detract from the centrality in the Church's life of faithful preaching, the celebration of the sacraments, the public reading of the Scriptures and the prayers, and from the closely-knit community life in church order which maintains and is sustained by these."[3] Jenkins believes that these are *the* characteristic church actions and as such should be known to be indispensable and to have primacy over other church actions. The second line of action prescribed by Jenkins seems at the outset a bit vague: " The Church and its faithful ministers, having done their best to ensure that the means of grace are available as readily as possible, will strive to keep the Church free from any encumbrances which might prevent it from coming to grips with the world about it."[4] Only as he elaborates his meaning do we begin to see how this line of action is radically different from much of the contemporary working concept of the ministry. " The minister will have to accept a role which is poles apart from that of the successful institutional promoter which is often regarded as normative by many of the flourishing churches of the West today. He may even have to incur the odium of some fellow-members of the Church in doing so. And he will spend a great deal of time and energy in helping his fellow-members see that it is as they approach their task in the world with humility, competence and perseverance that they best serve the Church. It is not easy for the chief executive officer of an institution to have the responsibility of constantly reminding its members that they are called to serve other things which are more important than the secular well-being of that institution, but the minister can approach this task with confidence because he cannot really proclaim the faith which he professes without understanding why this must be so and without seeing ways in which it can be so.

" There is no place where religion becomes the enemy of faith more obviously than where the Church becomes preoccupied with her own institutional stability and with defining her precise position as a centre of power over against the rest of society. . . . The whole art of churchmanship . . . consists in preventing the Church from becoming an end in itself and in preserving its instrumental character."[5]

This second line of action, Jenkins admits, seems at odds with the first, but he insists that each is essential to the other and to the church if the church is to survive. Then he adds a final note that may shed light on both the former: the church must devote far more time and money than it does on its equivalent of research and experiment. He elaborates this task as that of redefining the task of the church and its ministry and what may be termed their self-understanding. This redefinition involves theological thinking and rethinking, which is not being done. " The revival of Biblical study and of the study of some limited aspects of church history and the history of Christian doctrine which has taken place in our time should greatly assist the Church in this work of re-definition. It is, however, an example of the religious retreat from faith that, in modern England especially, concentration upon these is being used increasingly as a justification for avoiding the difficulties of the work of systematic theology through which alone that re-definition can be attempted.

" The need is no less urgent in relation to discovering a fresh style of life for the Church as a community in our own time. There are many thoughtful Protestants who are acutely dissatisfied with the forms of worship and with the patterns of community life of the churches of which they are members. It is often a mark of the Protestant who has seen some of the meaning of ' religionless Christianity ' that he has constantly to make up his mind on Sunday whether the irritation which he will experience if he goes to church is less intolerable than the sense of frustration and guilt he will have if he stays at home."[6]

These last sentences may suggest to us a deeper dimension of the problem than Jenkins has illuminated. Why should the " Protestant who has seen some of the meaning of ' religionless Christianity ' " have this continuing irritation upon attending Sunday church worship? With the religious revival, there has come a liturgical revival, and certainly evangelical orthodoxy and neoorthodoxy are not strangers to American pulpits, nor to British ones for that matter. Much of Jenkins' first line of action noted above is carried out more or less faithfully in many Sunday church worship services. We may be allowed to wonder at this point whether Jenkins' very insistence on the primacy and indispensability of these characteristic actions is not in some way related to the irritation experienced by the enlightened Christian.

A NEW LANGUAGE FOR THEOLOGY

The wonder expressed above leads us to the second theologically minded church leader who has penned a stinging critique of the church, John A. T. Robinson, the Bishop of Woolwich, England. Before we leave Jenkins, however, it should be noted that he is calling for a radical rethinking of the task of the church, its ministry and form, and of the theology that underlies these. In the main, then, his finger points at the local church and at the theologians, and at their interrelation or lack of it.

Robinson's book, *Honest to God*,[7] has achieved considerable popularity, if not notoriety, because it outlines in sharp, clear terms what he believes to be the cause of many Christians' disaffection with the church, viz., an outmoded theology. As he notes in his preface, although there are many, doubtless a majority at present, who see the best course as a " firm reiteration, in fresh and intelligent contemporary language, of ' the faith once delivered to the saints,' " he believes that " we are being called, over the years ahead, to far more than a restating of traditional orthodoxy in modern terms. . . . A much more radical recasting . . . is demanded, in the process of which the most fundamental categories of our theology—of God, of the supernatural, and of religion itself—must go into the melting. . . . For I am convinced that there is a growing gulf between the traditional orthodox supernaturalism in which our Faith has been framed and the categories which the ' lay ' world . . . finds meaningful today."[8]

The characteristic church actions prescribed by Jenkins are those most tightly tied to the traditional orthodox language that Robinson suspects of being unintelligible, if not downright incredible, to contemporary man because of his way of thinking about his world and himself. Further, Robinson emphasizes that he does not mean contemporary pagan man, but the solid Christian who occupies the pew regularly. The language of the pulpit in sermon and prayer, the sacramental language of the church, the hymns and responses with which the characteristic church actions are carried out, is a language forged within another world view than that which dominates the mind of man today. As Robinson sees it, the language of the Bible speaks of a God " up there," meaning literally *up*, and of Jesus literally ascending to sit at the right hand of God, and that such speaking " created no embarrassment—because it had not yet become a difficulty."[9] Most of us, says Robinson, are able to translate this notion of a God " up there " to one of a God " out there " beyond whatever limit to the universe there may be, or at least spiritually " out there." " But the signs are that we are reaching the point at which the whole conception of a God ' out there,' which has served us so well since the collapse of the three-decker universe, is itself becoming more of a hindrance than a help."[10] " But today I believe we may be confronted by a double crisis. The final psychological, if not logical, blow delivered by modern science and technology to the idea that there might *literally* be a God ' out there ' has *coincided* with an awareness that the *mental* picture of such a God may be more of a stumbling-block than an aid to belief in the Gospel. . . .

" But suppose such a super-Being ' out there ' is really only a sophisticated version of the Old Man in the sky? Suppose belief in God does not, indeed cannot, mean being persuaded of the ' existence ' of some entity, even a supreme entity, which might or might not be there, like life on Mars? Suppose the atheists are right—but that this is no more the end or denial of Christianity than the discrediting of the God ' up there,' which must in its time have seemed the contradiction of all that the Bible said? Suppose that all such atheism does is to destroy an idol, and that we can and must get on without a God ' out there ' at all? Have we seriously faced the possibility that to abandon such an idol may in the future be the only way of making Christianity meaningful? "[11]

Robinson has not only reemphasized Jenkins' point that the theological task of the church is crying out for attention; he has stated his conviction that a radical overhaul of the whole language of theology seems in order. Let us not forget, however, Jenkins' focus on the role of the ministry and the action of the local congregation. If we are to appreciate the real dimensions of the trouble in contemporary Christianity, the theological problem and the question of the nature and activity of the local congregation and its ministry must be held together.

A third writer, attacking the present situation in Christian ethics, also sheds some light upon the complexity of the problem. John Fry is convinced that Christian ethics is no longer speaking, nor even can speak, to the average man in the pew.

" When Christian ethics appears as the application of moral counsel to the problems encountered in modern life the ethicist assumes that the people who have these problems are going to heed the counsel and that the counsel is worth heeding. Neither assumption is ordinarily warranted by the realities. To fashion a ' problem ' out of an incredibly complicated and shifting situation, the ethicist must lop off or ignore purely individual and absolutely private factors of the situation. Nothing so grand as a problem is otherwise possible. And consider, also, the people who are alleged to have these problems. They may not be in an appropriate position for receiving and following the counsel. They may find the counsel unfollowable. They may be, candidly, unable to work out counseled solutions because of the most awesome and overlooked fact of all: they are immobilized.

" By constructing problems that he is supposed to have and then by offering counsel that he cannot abide, the Christian ethics ordinarily done today has missed the immobilized, private individual in the Christian public. Even sophisticated, very up-to-date Christian ethics has missed the immobilized, nameless, faceless individual."[12]

The individual Christian has been missed, thinks Fry, because his radical individuality, his personal daily phenomenal world, has been ignored. Not only that, but in its concern to be realistic, to speak to the power centers where decisions are actually made, Christian ethics has in fact, in thought and in language, "bypassed the Christian public, just as successful politics bypasses the voting public, and successful business bypasses the buying public. There is nothing snobbish or sinister in the bypass. The belief that a bypass is necessary is a function of the complexity itself. The whole public, or the whole Christian public, is too large, too plural, too inefficient to marshal and discharge power effectively. Therefore it is bypassed and presented with press releases, and the over-corrected but still rampant moralism."[13]

Fry adds that it is pointless to simplify the Christian ethics presently being formulated so that the Christian public may have available a clarified version, because it is not intended for the present powerless immobilized public that neither knows nor cares to know, neither acts nor cares to act in the realistic world of which and to which realistic Christian ethics speaks. The point clearly is that realistic Christian ethics is not so realistic after all, because it has not looked long or hard at the lonely individual, nor has it taken him and his personal world as its starting point.

"This talking that Christian ethics has lately been engaging in has not had him in mind. That is my contention. It has gone over his head. Therefore, I am suggesting here a sharply different, if not new, starting place for Christian ethics: that immobilized man out there. He is as all-by-himself as ever. He contains a complexity that keeps evading the categories of every single scientific analyst. What he is and where he stands just do not submit to any kind of definitive analysis. He is neither chartable, nor graphable, nor pollable. That is why, adopting this starting point, we shall have little use for any science available to conflow with the Christian faith. We want to begin with this immobilized man as he is *before* science takes over, where he lives, namely, in absolute, incontrovertible, majestic privacy. A prolegomena to any future Christian ethics is interested in this man, this Privacy, not for purposes of becoming effective at a later date, or in order to determine a suitable program that will mobilize him, but solely in the belief that what he actually does, feels, thinks, and believes constitutes the beginning place for any Christian ethics that will ever be done. And let's stop kidding ourselves."[14]

Fry thus proposes to begin with the individual immobilized man. His method is a phenomenological analysis of the interior world—the world that provides the only access to the actual world in which the individual lives; a world not describable by scientific methods of measurement and categorization and not particularly subject to prediction or control.

We have dealt at some length with Fry because the contention that he makes about ethics seems applicable also to the work of most Biblical scholars and theologians. They are speaking to and about a people who are by no means those occupying the pews of the churches. The language of these scholars is often scarcely understandable by their fellow scholars, and few pastors or parishioners even make a serious attempt to master their intricate prose. The complexity and the sheer length of the writings of some contemporary theologians put their work out of reach of any but professional theologians. Their works deserve the kind of clever spoofing that Stanley Romaine Hopper has given in a few pages of his excellent essay "The Modern Diogenes: A Kierkegaardian Crotchet."[15] It is probably not that theologians and Biblical scholars do not wish to speak to the man in the pew, but their very training and their world of professional associates make it all but impossible. Scholars are trained and habituated to write and think for scholars and to worry about what other scholars will say if they appear unscholarly. Such a system is supposed to bring about the best thinking possible, to motivate honesty, clarity, and rationality. Whether it does or does not is debatable, but it seems certain that one result of the system is the bypassing of the individual in the pew and a failure to grapple intimately or seriously with his world.

Three factors can be added together now to sharpen our picture of the trouble with the Christian churches in the second half of the twentieth century. There is something radically lacking in the image of the ministry and the local congregation; there is no viable pattern of thought by which to conceive the task and guide the action of the local congregation or the individual Christian. This lack is accompanied by a contemporary insistence on the performance of functions that have largely become meaningless or not understandable because they are cast in a language and world view far removed from that of contemporary man. Finally, those who might be expected to give some real thought to the entrapped situation of the man in the pew do their work in such an esoteric atmosphere that they have no real connection with him and his world so far as their professional thinking is concerned. It will be the endeavor of this book to set forth a theological foundation that does not bypass the individual, but rather takes his faith and language as its starting point and from that moves to discover the relation of the gospel to him and his faith-filled world with a view to setting forth a more suitable pattern for local church, theology, and their interrelation.

Chapter I

The Practice of Ministry and Theology

THEOLOGY has traditionally been divided into three task-oriented labor forces called exegetical theology, systematic theology, and practical theology. In the traditional schema, exegetical theology has concerned itself with the Biblical texts, their origin, setting, and grammar, with a view to establishing the meaning. Practical theology has dealt mainly with preaching, the expository presentation of a single text, the conduct of worship, and with other details of the pastoral ministry, sometimes descending to trivialities. Systematic theology alone has ranged across the whole horizon of Biblical texts and church tradition, comparing, contrasting, and trying to set forth the unity of the subject matter found therein. Although this has been the traditional division, individuals have ranged far from the pattern. Luther and Calvin, for example, worked equally well and equally hard in all three divisions. In our own day, some individuals are likewise far-ranging. Rudolf Bultmann, primarily an exegetical New Testament scholar, has set the world of systematic theology in great turmoil. Paul Tillich has probably communicated as much of his theology through published volumes of sermons as he has in his more systematic works. Thus the boundaries have always in some sense been more theoretical than actual, but they do represent the concentration of interest and thought of the persons laboring in the respective areas. In this latter fashion, the traditional schema has encouraged a wide split between the theologizing and the practice of the church. If, as is popularly supposed among scholars, the theology of the parish is twenty-five years behind that of the scholars, then the traditional schema must bear some of the blame for it.

Other important facts of modern church history also call into question the traditional task-oriented divisions of theology. Two such are of primary importance: the rise of the movement now known as Christian education, and the lay movement.

The actual rootages of Christian education are varied and debatable, depending on how one defines that which he is asking about. As currently identified more or less with Sunday church school instruction, however, it is intimately related with an intellectual awakening of the general public and a theological protest, both of which rose to significance in the eighteenth century. After the actual work of Reformation had subsided, theology in all its tasks became increasingly brittle and sterile. Exegetical theology was limited to textual and grammatical study of the revealed truth contained in the Holy Text. All texts of the Bible stood on equal ground, for all alike were the Word of God, as though spoken directly by him. Systematic theology was increasingly a matter of conserving the abstract once-for-all revealed truths as preserved in Bible and creeds. The task was too often conceived as merely organizing the revealed truths and deducing conclusions from them. Practical theology was engaged in seeking the most direct methods for preaching the revealed truths and systematic theology's system, and instruction was conceived as indoctrination. In all its tasks, theology conceived itself as mainly engaged in transmission of known facts and thus was essentially conservative and uncreative.

Fortunately, these were not the only fruits of Reformation thought. Along with the conviction that the church was responsible to be pure in doctrine, there was a realization that the church never had been and would never be wholly pure in doctrine. For this reason the church could not be allowed simply to settle into Reformed dogmatic ruts, but must ever be about the business of reforming. This spirit, though partially responsible for some of the tragic divisions in the Protestant communion, was also a lasting basis for the necessary freedom to engage in theology. Without this conviction that the last word has never been said, the conservative tide in theology in the eighteenth century might have dominated the whole of Protestantism, as it nearly did. Along with this conviction that the church must ever be reforming went another: the conviction that religion is something more than a matter of the mind, more than an intellectual statement of doctrine; it is a matter of heart and daily life. It is not simply that doctrine must be held with passion and be lived out, but that theology itself is not simply an intellectual task. Theologizing does not mean merely exegeting Scripture by scholarly rule and organizing the results into a system; it means listening with one's whole life and trying to say what it is that one hears. Nor is this listening a solitary task for a lonely soul who eschews the company of man for that of ancient volumes, but one listens in all the living patterns of life as well, and in the company of the faithful.

The conviction that swelled into life in the eighteenth century, and more fully in the nineteenth, was that expressed in an earlier day by saying the final authority for one's life was neither Bible nor Pope, but the inner testimony of the Holy Spirit. From the depths there was coming forth the understanding that God is the *living* God who works in his world *today,* just as he has always done and to whose living activity man can and does respond. This conviction was an assurance that the gospel was meant for man, that it was meant to be understandable. From this conviction and its evangelical zeal, the nineteenth-century liberal movement in theology gained what Henry P. Van Dusen has called its " central intellectual motive: to make Christian faith *intelligible* and *credible,* comprehensible *and* convincing to intelligent, informed, and honest minds of each successive era."[16] It is important that we note the evangelical zeal that was behind this intellectual conviction, for both aspects play a central role in the continuing vitality of this theological movement. This movement has had various fruit, good and not so good, but its central convictions are correct and were grossly lacking in much church life of then and now.

THE RISE OF GENERAL EDUCATION
AND THE SUNDAY SCHOOL

Parallel with and sharing some of the origins of liberal theology were general education and the Sunday school. The two latter movements share a common rootage in their conviction of the worth of social service and the importance of education for the welfare of the individual and the community, whether church or state. The Sunday school began and remained largely a lay movement. This fact is both its glory and its tragedy. The task of theological education, except in theological seminaries, has never been accepted by the church as being equally vital to its life with preaching or performing the Sacraments. Such understanding is still widespread today. " Very widely the task of the minister is conceived as primarily that of a preacher and pastor. If he carries any educational responsibility, that is something added which does not properly belong to his office. He does it only because his church cannot afford an educational director or because he cannot find laymen who will accept the full responsibility. He escapes from it at the earliest opportunity that he may concentrate upon what he considers his essential functions. Under heavy pressure, if any duty has to be dropped or left with scant attention, it is the educational one. When asked why they do not have classes for the training of teachers, ministers invariably answer that there is no time for them. They would not excuse themselves from preaching or from administering the sacraments or from any of the other essential functions of their ministry with a plea of 'no time.' Yet here they do so without any qualms, for to them the educational function is not essential to their ministry. Many theological seminaries in their curriculums mirror this defective conception of the ministry. They are organized for the training of a ministry that will be almost exclusively homiletic and pastoral and in which education is not expected to have much place."[17]

Several factors seem to have worked together to produce this tragic separation between the ministry of the church and the educational task of the church. In its origin, the Sunday school was not a part of the church, but was the effort of Christian people to give education to poor children who worked every other day of the week. It began and remained largely a lay movement that existed alongside the Sunday worship of the church. It focused mostly on children in its origin, and the stereotype has remained that all the work of education is that with children. The leaders and workers of the Sunday

school movement, however, knew almost instinctively
that something vital was involved and they refused to allow it to die. Thus, when it could not find a home within
the church, it was carried on apart from the church. We
may note here a connection with certain convictions expressed in the radical wing of the Reformation concerning
the part laymen are to play in the church. Luther had
enunciated clearly the priesthood of all believers as meaning that the whole church is called into the ministry, not
just the clergy: "We are all priests"; but he was never
able to implement fully his conviction.[18] Grimes, in his
recent work on the laity, indicates that it was the conviction of the radicals that "there were not, strictly speaking,
clergy and laity, but only believers, all of whom were to
assume full responsibility for the Christian community
even though they appointed officers who exercised special
functions."[19] Historically, the layman was to continue this
effort to be a responsible, informed member of the church
and of society, and one of the means that seemed to assist
him was the Sunday school. In the nineteenth century,
Sunday school outposts for decades were the first manifestation of the church in new communities or forsaken
places and served more often than not as the nucleus for
a local congregation. Generations of local laymen found
their spiritual life and growth most fostered by their ac-
tivities in this work.

Nevertheless, early in the nineteenth century, the Sunday school was shut out as far as the main-line churches
were concerned; but it was not without friends. A common enemy often makes strangers into friends, and thus
it was that the Sunday school became allied with the
evangelical churches, the followers of Wesley and White-
field. As James Smart notes: "As a consequence of this
alliance the Sunday School became strongly anchored in
the tradition of the evangelical revival. This influence is

to be traced in the conception of its purpose as an instrument for evangelizing the young, the character of the hymns associated with it which did so much to fix its tone, and also the theology which was long to be dominant in it, often in sharp antithesis to the theology of the Church in which the particular Sunday School had its home."[20]

The development of general education in the nineteenth century was marked with two salient characteristics: First, it was part and parcel of man's increasing rejection of authority, from whatever source, and his emphasis on autonomy. Democracy and reason were in the ascendancy. Man had faith in his ability to control his own destiny and in his right to do so. Second, in the nineteenth century there was a series of battles concerning religion in the public schools in America and the solution was reached—which has remained and continues—that religion was not to be taught by the state. This solution left the problem of religious instruction solely up to the church, and it may be fairly said that the Protestant Church generally has poorly recognized the task and has offered rather meager solutions.

HORACE BUSHNELL

One of the men in whom the ferment of liberal theology was at work and who was most sensitive to the need for the church to give attention to the problem of religious education as it was forced out of the public schools was Horace Bushnell. Bushnell was the pastor of a local church in Connecticut. As he pondered on the significance of the gospel for human life, he realized that orthodox theology not only was not directed to a certain section of humanity but was positive in its exclusion of that section from a relationship of faith in God. That portion of humankind called children was declared " to reject God and all holy principle " until mature, and to be " old enough to resist

all good, but too young to receive any good whatever,"
old enough to be damned, but not old enough to be saved.
"What opinion is more essentially monstrous, in fact,
than that which regards the Holy Spirit as having no
agency in the immature souls of children who are growing up, helpless and unconscious, into the perils of
time? "[21]

In 1847 Bushnell published his first tract attacking this
obvious evil and the theology that supported it. He was
reflecting back to theology and theologians from the world
of reality what he found there, and calling the theologians
to look with him at the practical effects of their doctrines
and not merely at their theoretical formulations. He was
saying to the local church, especially to parents, that they
had a responsibility to proclaim an intelligible gospel to
all people, not just adults. Why posit adolescent or adult
conversion as the only way into Christian faith? Why not
bring children up in Christian faith, in conversion?[22] To
implement such a task, Bushnell proposed a radically
Christian home as the mainstay, but his writings indicate
a strongly favorable attitude toward the Sunday school as
well.

Bushnell's protest was both theological and method-
ological, i.e., relating to the practices of the local church;
these are, as Bushnell realized, inseparable parts of one
whole. Although his protest was in the name of the children, it stemmed from the conviction that the gospel is
meant to be understood. He saw far better than some
dogmatically minded Christians do today that the gospel
can be proclaimed in a responsible and meaningful way
to any age group. He noted the need to translate into the
thought world of the child whatever it was that one
wanted to teach. Teachers should " begin with a kind of
teaching suited to the age of the child. First of all they
should rather seek to teach a feeling than a doctrine, to

bathe the child in their own feeling of love to God, and dependence on him, and contrition for wrong before him, bearing up their child's heart in their own, not fearing to encourage every good motion they call into existence; to make what is good, happy and attractive, what is wrong, odious and hateful."[23]

Bushnell was also surprisingly aware of pressures that have now been elaborated in psychoanalytic and socio-psychological theories. He observed the errors of the radical individualism of the theology of his day and elaborated what he called the organic nature of the state, the church, and the family.[24] His writings show that he was well aware of the unconscious power that these various groups have upon the individual, and in particular how a person's family literally molds his character. If anything, he put more stress upon the family than it can or should bear, but it must be remembered that in his day the family was much more unified and there were far fewer outside influences (such as the mass media) than there are today.

Bushnell consistently appealed both to the Bible and to reason, in the sense of inner conviction of truth, rather than using the Bible alone. He stood with the radical wing of the Reformation in his view that the layman has an indispensable part in the ongoing life of the church. The layman is not merely the consumer of the product that theologians or ministers devise; he is the church! If there is faith, it lives in him and his household. The church is not a purveyor of dogma; it is a household of faith.

THE RISE OF THE RELIGIOUS EDUCATION MOVEMENT

In the situation of declining religious instruction in the public schools, it was natural for the Sunday school movement to gain impetus. The last half of the nineteenth century may well be termed the era of the Sunday school.

Run largely by laymen, ill-equipped, lacking proper books
or meeting places, without skilled leadership at any level,
the Sunday school was nonetheless the place where hun-
dreds of thousands of people were given whatever religious instruction they received. Its glory was that it did
a job the institutional church and its clergy were neglecting; its tragedy was that the job was done poorly for the
most part. It was largely riddled with atrocious theology,
highly moralistic in tone. Because it was not welcome in
the main-line churches and found help almost solely from
churches of the evangelical wing, the Sunday school took
over the theological ideas of these churches, a naïve
orthodoxy, Biblical literalism, and too often, the revivalist
emphasis on conversion. Its teaching materials were
heavily weighted on memory work, especially the Bible.
There was no significant difference in the lesson as taught
to six-year-olds or to twelve-year-olds. It is perhaps not
unfair to say that the Sunday school movement learned
nothing from the fields of Biblical or theological studies,
nothing from the writings of Bushnell, and nothing from
the progress being made in public schools in educational
methodology.

Obviously, all this wooden-headedness was not going
unnoticed. Many laymen and clergy were well enough
informed to know that a housecleaning was in order. The
mark of the beginning of a new era came with the found-
ing of the Religious Education Association in 1903. This
group was largely motivated by its awareness of the poor
job that the Sunday school was doing and it was, in the
main, a group of laymen. Despite its good intentions, the
Religious Education Association had a fatal flaw, well
described by James Smart. " In its early years, one of the
primary aims of the Association was to stimulate a more
scholarly use of the Bible. Those who gathered at Chicago,

however, were united more by their consciousness of the inadequacy of the Sunday School and their desire for a new day in religious education than by their adherence to any one theological point of view. How divergent the conceptions of religion could be is shown by the fact that one speaker of the convention was John Dewey, who certainly had a different understanding of the word ' religion ' from that of those who were so anxious for a revived influence of the Bible in the Church. Theologically, the Religious Education Association, both at this time and later, was content to be nebulous. It committed itself to no theology, since it desired to unite all those who were working for a more intelligent approach to problems of religious education, both in the Church and beyond the Church. Never did a movement face a clearer need or begin with greater enthusiasm, but, because it shared, with the earlier Sunday School movement, a loose and indecisive relationship with the Church, and because it assumed falsely that the theological question could be ignored, it was never to fulfill the promise of its beginnings or to do for the Church educationally what needed so badly to be done."[25]

THE EVANGELICAL MINISTER AND THEOLOGY

The ministry in America at the opening of the nineteenth century was patterned largely upon that of the Puritan age in England, modified by " evangelicalism." Whatever profound understanding and heritage the ministry had seems due mainly to the Puritan tradition, but an exceedingly large amount of adaptation was taking place. Changes were made as rapidly as the frontier situation seemed to demand and were equally promptly justified by demonstrating them to be in perfect harmony with Biblical teaching or apostolic practices. Sidney Mead suggests that, although American ministers were constantly adjusting the form of the ministry so that it bore little resemblance to traditional patterns, they were so woodenly Biblicistic that they continually insisted they were only returning to pristine apostolic practices.[26]

Tradition actually exerted little influence in America upon most of the ministers of the early nineteenth century and later. They took pride in being Protestants, which to them meant freedom from the restraint of tradition. Further, for the most part, they had been little exposed to tradition beyond that of serving in an apprentice capacity to another minister. A strange divorce had taken place between intellectual endeavor and the practice of the ministry. Pietism had so permeated the Protestant Church with its emphasis on personal religious experience and holiness of life as the essence of the Christian life that intellectual effort or appeal to reason seemed of dubious value. Education for the ministry under the pietistic emphasis stressed the conversion of the soul and not the training of the mind. In the local churches these views led to increasing emphasis on revivalistic practices. The task of the ministry was conceived as soul-saving, and the success or failure of a minister was too often based on his ability to bring about conversions. It was even believed by many that the religious state of the minister was the major factor in his ability to convert others. In this way, theological training and understanding were more and more removed from being essential qualifications for the minister to an indifferent and finally negative value for many groups. Under this emphasis, the usual minister became less and less critical of the peculiar tradition of the denomination in which he served and tended to a dogmatic assertion of the delivered version of Protestantism as he received it.

The same trend away from intellectual endeavor can be seen in the abandoning of the teaching aspect of the ministry. It is clear from descriptions of the ministry in the Puritan age that instruction in doctrine and practice was a large part of the ministry. Sermons were then an important teaching device, as they had been for Calvin and Luther. In the Presbyterian Church, for example, the minister was (and still is) called a teaching elder as his major title. Ministers were expected to teach both children and adults in the faith, and a pastoral visit was a theological examination for the whole family.

With the tide of evangelicalism, however, teaching increasingly seemed less and less important. When so great an emphasis is put on the conversion of the soul, it is easy to forget subsequent needs and allow oneself to be totally absorbed in working for conversions. More and more the task of the ministry was geared to bringing men to decision. The rise of the Sunday school further allowed the assumption that some provision was actually being made for the education of the children of the church, and that this was in any case a job for the layman. " Expositions of the Word tended to be supplemented by application of the Word to the consciences of men for immediate decision. Of the three parts of the usual sermon in the previous period—exegesis of a text, laying down of the doctrine, and application—the third almost crowded out the other two. Even as learned and sober an adviser to ministers as J. A. James by implication belittled the first as ' a meatless, marrowless bone of criticism,' the second as ' a dry crust of philosophy,' and extolled the third as ' the bread which cometh down from heaven.' "[27]

The image of the minister as the revivalist, or soul saver, gives little impetus to theological study, and as we have noted, the major theological knowledge of the American ministry of the evangelical type in the first half of the nineteenth century was an emotionalized version of their own denominational orthodoxy. Such a thin and uncritical theological knowledge provides no base at all for the intellectual give-and-take that is necessary for creative theological effort. Emphasis on denominational truth led to a rigid orthodoxy that in turn had a further deleterious effect upon the minister as teacher. If one begins with an assumption that he has in his possession the "truth once for all delivered to the saints," he cannot but understand education in a transmissive sense. Education in this way is believed to be the transmission of revealed truths. Such a view can put complete faith in a catechetical teaching and in memory work; orthodoxy can be reduced to a series of statements to be memorized. No great knowledge or skill is needed for teaching material of this type; hence the minister can allow others to do this work while he tries to convert the lost.

A further effect of this thin theological base is to make one less resistant to the pull and push of cultural patterns and ideals when these are at odds with Christianity. Under such circumstances it is all too easy to identify God and country, Christian ethics and social mores. The actions of some American ministers with respect to slavery, the Civil War, and World War I give numerous examples of this weakness. The support of slavery and its justification on Biblical grounds is a chapter in the history of the church no more savory than the Inquisition. The attitudes and actions of many Northern ministers after the Civil War who looked upon the South as mission territory and who treated even their Southern ministerial brethren as infidels did nothing to further the ministry of reconciliation. Nor did ministers who championed World War I as " God's War " to make the world " safe for democracy " demonstrate an understanding of the God whose love is for the world without exception and who commands the love of one's enemy.

THEOLOGY AND THE LIBERAL MINISTER

As we have noted, the impact of the Enlightenment can be seen in America in various ways, one of them being the rise of general education. Among the evangelical ministry the thought of the Enlightenment found little root, but it was not so in Europe. There, some ministers and theologians sensed that the reason which the Enlightenment proclaimed was not to be despised as a Promethean rebellion against God, but as an awareness of the principles of justice and truth and goodness, a loyalty to the spirit of truth that is identified with the Spirit of God. The Enlightenment for them was an attempt to base social and political structures upon a trust that there was a grand harmony running through all of life, so that if man were free to pursue truth, this harmony would itself give order to all their affairs. Democracy is one expression of this trust. Nor were the leading thinkers of the Enlightenment naïve enough to believe that this truth would always be represented by the ideas of the majority; hence it had a strong conviction that there must be tolerance. Out of this ground in Europe, liberal theology arose. In its origin, it is found in the German Enlightenment, stemming from the work of Lessing, the poet and philosopher; David F. Strauss, a critical Biblical scholar; and Friedrich Schleiermacher, a theological apostle to the intellectual skeptics of his day. It was not many decades in crossing the Atlantic.

It is not possible or necessary here to trace the theological history of the nineteenth century. It will be enough to mention briefly a man who set much of the tone for a century of theological thought, and then move to one aspect of that thought which immediately preceded the theological revival of the twentieth century. Friedrich Schleiermacher was thirty-two years old and an established preacher when the nineteenth century made its debut. Educated by the Moravian Brethren, he always held something of their understanding of the relation between man and God. Convinced of the necessity for everyone to enter this relationship to God in order truly to find fulfillment, Schleiermacher was greatly disturbed by the lack of appeal that Protestant scholastic theology had for the educated classes. His analysis of Christianity led him to the conviction that its essence was a feeling or sense of dependence upon the transcendent All and a sense of unity with the All. Out of this experience, there arises a sense of personal worth. Morally each person represents mankind in his own particular way, but this takes place within a social context. The individual is to work with others for the establishment of a better order of things. His basic optimism about man and his evangelical concern were destined to be carried forward in that movement of theology known as liberalism.

In America, evangelical Protestantism was clearly becoming the dominant church ethos until the Darwinian theory of evolution and the rapidly rising scientific movement took root in America and brought a new development. Soon after the mid-nineteenth century, a sharp reaction away from simple evangelicalism appeared among the Protestant ministry that soon developed into the liberal movement. From its evangelical background liberalism retained a strong impetus to proclaim the gospel to those who had not heard, but from its sources in the Enlightenment it had a drive to be heard intellectually as well as emotionally. With the Sunday school and general education, liberalism shared a social and educational concern that was to issue in the social gospel and make liberalism a natural companion to the religious education movement.

Liberalism was in reaction against a sterile and uncritical theological attitude that clung to the dogmas of the past, and it was aware that the ministry must engage in theology as its very own task that could not simply be relegated to the authority of theologians or the traditions of the past. As Henry Ward Beecher put it in his *Yale Lectures on Preaching:* " You cannot go back and become apostles of the dead past, driveling after ceremonies, and letting the world do the thinking and studying. There must be a new spirit infused into the ministry."[28] Among the liberals, Biblical literalism had no place, nor did they feel it always necessary to justify their practices on the basis of Biblical texts or apostolic practice. Past practices and past creeds ceased to be rigid boundaries and became historical items to be reinterpreted and rewritten for the contemporary man. A high value was placed on education for the minister, and most liberal ministers were well educated.

Many liberal ministers were set in urban parishes and there exposed to the vice, crime, disease, poverty, and human waste of the slum and the relation of these to overwork, low pay, unemployment, and ignorance. These men soon involved themselves in various efforts to improve conditions. Given their intellectual bent and the freedom to theologize, many of them set out to analyze the nature of these ills and to ask what the church could and should do about them. Such efforts gave birth to a new and uniquely American theology, the social gospel, whose major architect was Walter Rauschenbusch. The men who formed the social gospel movement were not afraid to involve themselves and the churches they served with the particular plight of the poor and the outcast of their day, trying to show what it meant really to love the world.

Liberal theology, however, had its own fatal flaws. In its anxiety to be relevant, to proclaim a credible gospel, it sometimes slipped into what may be called the modernist heresy, which adjusts Bible and doctrine to fit the assumptions and dogmas of contemporary thought. In its love of man and its trust in rational thought, liberal theology frequently was overoptimistic about man's ability to do good and to think clearly, and quite uncritical of his ability to do evil and to rationalize any behavior. In these ways it at times ceased to be theology at all and became a sort of philosophical moralism, or worse, a romantic moralism. Nonetheless, liberal theology at its best was a movement of great power and insight, one that deserves careful study. At its heart is the correct conviction that theology is a handmaiden to the gospel, that the task of theology is to communicate the one gospel to the contemporary mind. We may add here, theology must not forget to come to grips with tradition in its anxiety to communicate, nor may it avoid taking seriously the situation of contemporary man by preoccupying itself with tradition.

THE RISE OF FUNDAMENTALISM

Evangelical Protestantism was put on the defensive by the rising tide of science and liberal theology and its response was, as someone has said, a hardening of the categories. It began to reiterate and reemphasize ever more rigidly and uncritically its secondhand seventeenth-century dogmas. By the beginning of the twentieth century, it had hardened into fundamentalism. Robert

Michaelsen says that fundamentalism had five major characteristics: " (1) vigorous resistance to developments in the world of science that appeared to contradict the Biblical text; (2) Biblical literalism; (3) individualism; (4) moralism; and (5) insistence on belief in certain 'fundamentals' such as the inerrancy of the Scriptures, the virgin birth of Jesus Christ, and his second coming."[29] Much of the energy and creative potential of fundamentalism went into its battle against what it considered the enemies of God and the true gospel, i.e., science and liberal theology. The fundamentalist minister made common ground with the Sunday school because he saw it in terms of its evangelical theology and its willingness to work for the conversion of children. He saw little need for any more serious form of religious education, since he was conversion-minded and questioned the value of education in general.

Fundamentalism is as much an attitude, a psychology, as it is an honest theological conviction. In its psychology it represents an effort to achieve security and certainty. Its beginning point is composed of one or more dogmatic statements about the Bible and about Jesus' relation to God, which then become the basis for an assurance that anything the Bible says is literally true, and this latter statement in turn supports the previous dogma about Jesus; the circular argument is thus complete.

The poignancy and naïveté of fundamentalism are suggested by a discussion between a young preministerial student and his gray-haired philosophy professor.

STUDENT: " Sir, I am sure that Jesus was more than just a man; the Bible itself tells us that he was the Son of God and prayer is offered to him."

PROFESSOR: " Of course. But suppose one thought the Biblical writers at this point were simply incorrect."

STUDENT: " Why, sir, they can't be! Jesus called himself the Son of God! "

PROFESSOR: " Suppose he actually did, does that make it true, just because he said so? What if he was mistaken? "

The student's world was shaken not a little. Indeed, the cold fact suddenly came home to him; *Jesus could have been mistaken.* In a flash the absolute venture that faith is was thrust upon him as the comfortable security of intellectual certainty vanished.

The tragedy of fundamentalism is that it wants to *believe it knows* the truth more than it *wants to know* the truth. In this blind determination that it knew the truth, it continued the misbegotten war against science and liberal theology to its logical and absurd conclusion, the Scopes trial of 1925, which featured the famous politician and Sunday school leader William Jennings Bryan defending the faith of fundamentalism and famous trial lawyer Clarence Darrow defending the defendant. Although Bryan won the case, he clearly lost the battle, and the power of fundamentalism began to decline.

Chapter II

Theology and Ministry
in the Twentieth Century

IT IS ONLY as one grasps the basic mental outlook that
pervaded Western civilization at the turn of the century that one can appreciate the developments that have
taken place since then. We may characterize that period
by saying that progress was the keynote and science was
the demigod. If one does not wish to call science a god,
one would at least be willing to admit that science was the
means by which man proposed to reach the desired end
for his life. Man then felt that he knew where he wanted
to go and he believed that science was the way to get
there. The industrial revolution was in full bloom and
man almost universally believed its promise of conquer-
ing poverty and of delivering man from the ills, the difficulties, and the pressures of life that had been his from
time immemorial in this world. Early in the century, it
appeared to man that if he could extend education widely
enough, then he could expect a rule of rationality to per-
vade the world. Man believed that if only all mankind
were educated well and properly, then they would think
clearly, and by thinking clearly, they would govern themselves wisely and well. War was soon to be outlawed, for
indeed all civilized men already realized that war was a
ridiculous and a morbid way of settling the affairs of mankind. It was believed that modern man in his wisdom had

outgrown war. The application of the scientific method was expected to solve man's social problems as well as his physical problems on every side of life.

One of the interesting aspects of this period can be seen by reviewing the statements made by Christian leaders of the time. One finds that they frequently expressed an unbelievably naïve optimism that war would soon be ended and that the Kingdom of God would in fact be seen within the social order of man. Washington Gladden, a theological liberal, spoke many times with this fantastic optimism, and his sermons are a valuable insight into the mental attitude of the period. At one point Gladden expressed considerable regret because he felt that his age would not permit him to live another twenty or thirty years; he felt that if he could live just this much longer, he would surely see the presence of the Kingdom of God. This particular statement was made in the year 1908; it is ironical that only six years later the world began to be buried in the cataclysm of World War I. Further insight into the naïveté of the times may be seen by examining what was meant for the most part when preachers of that day spoke of the Kingdom of God. For them the Kingdom of God was a state of social affairs. It was that state in which people took care of their neighbors, in which medicine and other techniques, such as social science and politics, would make it possible to live together in a glorious and glamorous organized society. The point is that the Kingdom of God was understood as a social organization; this is clearly not in harmony with what the Bible speaks about as seeking the Kingdom of God. In the Bible, the Kingdom of God is that state of life in which God is one's King. A more adequate, or at least more easily understood, translation for the Kingdom of God would be to speak of it as the Reign of God or the Kingship of God.

Various means were envisaged for bringing in the Kingdom of God. The first was social action or social gospel, which was to penetrate both labor and business and through which the downtrodden were to be aided. The advent of the social gospel, of course, did issue in the betterment of labor-business relationships and in an increasing social-mindedness on the part of government as well as private institutions. Care for the sick, the aged, and the underprivileged owes an incredible debt to the social gospel movement of this time. A second major thrust was that of mission activity. One theory behind the mission movement was that if people in the areas of the world that were not Christian could be converted, then assuredly all would be well, for if all people were Christians, then surely the social order would be right. Nonetheless, despite the gains, the very real gains, that came about through the social gospel and the mission emphasis, optimism was destined to come crashing down and to be followed by the almost total hopelessness that pervades much of the world today.

The Religious Education Association to a considerable degree shared the optimistic mood of this period, even where it was strangely mated with a Calvinistic theology. This new movement was soon branded an enemy of the gospel by the evangelical-orthodox wing of the church, because it did not subscribe to literalism in Biblical interpretation, nor indoctrination with orthodox dogmas as its educational method, but tried to work for an intelligent approach to the interpretation of Scripture and the problems of education. Finding itself shut out by the evangelicals, the movement drifted rather naturally into the camp of the liberals. As indicated earlier, the Religious Education Association was and still is officially neutral in theology, but this neutrality makes it often seem no more than a movement concerned with educational method-

ology. As will become clearer, however, in a later chapter
on the nature of faith, philosophical and theological
neutrality are impossible. In educational methodology,
one expresses the logical outcome of his presuppositions,
and these latter reflect theological and philosophical convictions.

The theological-philosophical convictions that stand
out most clearly in the religious educators of the age of
optimism are those which also are found in the general
educators of the time, viz., growth and guidance of
growth in persons. George A. Coe summed up his theory
of religious education in a statement that clearly displays
these elements. Religious education, he said, " is the systematic, critical examination and reconstruction of relations between persons guided by Jesus' assumptions that
persons are of infinite worth, and by the hypothesis of the
existence of God, the great Valuer of persons."[30] In the
practice of Christian education, Coe rigorously applied
the principles of social psychology to gain the maximum
" growth " of persons. He did not, however, raise radically
the question of the ultimate value of growth or how we
know it to be valuable. Further, his statement of the
nature of growth is developed upon the basis of social
psychology and is left unrelated to theology.

William Clayton Bower continued the line of thought
that assumes man's ability to control his future for good
and which proposes to educate people who will then be
suited to carry out this task. " When through expanding
knowledge and increasing control of his world, man becomes self-conscious and self-determining, he enters with
intelligence and purpose into cooperation with these external forces, and in a large measure, creates his own
future, and the future of his institutions. When man
arrives at this point he becomes, in the deepest and most

spiritual sense, a worker together with God in the ongoing life of the world."[31]

THE END OF OPTIMISM

The end of the optimistic period in Europe is marked by the beginning of World War I. European civilization, widely pervaded, in its intellectual levels at least, by naïve optimism, was shaken to its roots by the events of the First World War, in which the most highly advanced nations of the world fought one another as if the battlefield were the final measuring rod of truth. A man who exemplified in himself the crushing blow that World War I was to Western civilization was Stefan Zweig, a well-known intellectual and an Eastern European writer. Zweig said that the world had been torn from under him by World War I and that he was too old to start over again. He recognized that the events of World War I meant literally that one *had* to start all over again, for the rabid optimism of the world before that day was not adequate for the new world that had come to be as a result of the war. He could not begin again, and his life ended in suicide. In America, World War I was not sufficient to end optimism, but the great depression and World War II, which followed soon after it, put an end to all the rosy dreams, rosy dreams which believed that every day in every way the world was getting better and better.

The "this-worldly" optimism of the roaring twenties came to an end with the thrifty thirties. In the roaring twenties the opinion was that the purpose of life was to have a good time, to live it up, and people did. Suddenly, however, it was all taken away from them, and a whole way of life came to an end. And they, like Stefan Zweig, realized that life had no meaning and they asked themselves how they were to go on. Many of them, of course, were not able to go on and they too committed suicide. Others, when they reflected upon it, realized not only that life had no meaning now but that it had had no meaning for them even when they were well-to-do financially. With wealth gone, at least for the moment, something else was discovered for which to hope. That was the hope of building a better world, a brighter and more glorious tomorrow. And this kind of hope was very common in the 1930's in America and filled the heart of every good young red-blooded American boy who felt that his life would be meaningful through building a bigger and better tomorrow. After the events of World War II made their impact upon America, this second kind of starry optimism began to wane. It was at last becoming clear that not within any one or even many lifetimes would we be able to build a better, happier, and more glorious society.

What were the events that so thoroughly eliminated the naïve optimism that had lasted even through the great depression? First of all, no one failed to notice that a highly civilized, perhaps the most thoroughly cultured nation on the face of the earth, found itself able to murder six million Jews. These people were murdered for no reason other than that they were Jews. The country that did this was not backward; it was not underprivileged; it did not lack in education; its science of all varieties led almost every other nation in the world; its universities were models for all to imitate. Furthermore, this nation had a long history of Christianity. Still other nations that were determined to " rise," as they interpreted that word, destroyed millions of people who rejected their ideology; these latter remarks are directed, of course, to Russia, and in later years to China, where those who stand in the way of the contemporary ideology are to be destroyed.

Yet the first decade of this century saw an almost universal conviction that this century would see the spread of parliamentary government, of democracy to all the nations of the world.

Today it seems, for the new nations that are rising up and for those nations that are in a hurry to reach the pinnacle of power, that the last word in government is dictatorship rather than democracy. It is the conviction of these nations that dictatorship will take them from where they are to where they want to go in the quickest way possible. Another factor that is detrimental to any kind of optimism is the explosive nature of the nationalism of the younger nations. Whether one considers Africa or South America or Asia, it is apparent that many of the younger nations are running along virtually out of control. It is indeed possible that a new nation of which one has never heard will start a local war that could spread into World War III and bring about the destruction of all civilization on the earth. The final, and for thinking people perhaps the conclusive, blow to optimism is the discovery that freedom for the individual, which was the keystone of the old democracies, is a vanishing commodity even here in these United States of America. It is an incredible, but all too evident, phenomenon to see freedom and liberty being reduced in the name of freedom and liberty, yet this takes place here and now. These various facts have made it exceedingly difficult, if not totally impossible, for one to be optimistic about tomorrow bringing a better world.

THE RELIGIOUS REVIVAL

First, let us give our attention to the religious revival in the United States located approximately in time from 1940 to 1958. These years saw many strange events, and within the church one of them was an almost unaccountable rise in membership. Churches that were not engaging in any effort to increase their membership found their services being better attended and discovered new people asking to be allowed to unite with that particular congregation. By the mid-1940's it was evident that a great religious revival of some kind was under way in the United States. For the years 1940 to 1958, the membership rolls of the church showed a great—indeed a very great—increase, substantially exceeding in percentage the population growth of the United States as a whole. It was thus that the late '40's and the '50's were an era of institutional expansion and building such as had never been seen before in America. In the decade of the 1950's, theological seminaries found it impossible to train ministers in sufficient quantity to fill the available posts. In fact, new churches were coming into existence almost rapidly enough to use up the entire output of the seminaries. In dozens of suburban situations, buildings literally could not be erected rapidly enough to accommodate the people who came rushing to knock on the door of the church. Two and three Sunday morning worship services and Sunday schools were often necessary. Presumably these people were coming to hear what the church had to say.

As early as 1950 many questions were being raised about the true significance of this religious revival. Some people were saying that it was only a foxhole kind of religion; others declared that America was spiritually coming of age; still others attempted to explain it totally in terms of sociology. Within the church, although many were asking whether the revival would last and whether it had any real depth to it, the major reaction was simply to take it at face value and attempt to do whatever could be done with the rush of people.

In the years 1959 to 1961, something new began to appear in religious statistics: the rate of growth slowed up.

In fact, in 1961 it had slowed up to such an extent that the Protestant Church was no longer growing as rapidly as the population as a whole. The growth rate of the Protestant Church in particular had shot up precipitately soon after the onset of World War II. The growth rate continued upward, leveling off sometime in the early 1950's, but now the rate of growth of the Protestant Church has decreased until it is actually less than the rate of growth of the population. Even more, people are not now joining the Protestant Church in numbers as large as children being born to Protestant families. It is doubtless too early to make even reasonable guesses as to what the meaning of this change in rate of growth may be. No one at this time can be certain whether or not this is an omen for the future, meaning that the Protestant Church is to decline in the next few years. The fact that this phenomena is accompanied by declining enrollments in most of the Protestant theological seminaries does give pause for thought, however. If nothing else, the Protestant Church is in for a time of serious reevaluation of itself. The kind of naïve optimism about the growth of the church that was reflected in the yearly slogan for one great denomination, " A Million More in '54 and Every Member a Tither," is no longer possible in the face of these facts. In order to see the religious revival and its demise in better perspective, however, let us look at the theological revival.

THE THEOLOGICAL REVIVAL

The birthplace of the theological revival about which we speak may well be said to have been the pulpit of Karl Barth. Barth found himself in a situation in which he began to raise questions about his preaching, and whether or not it was meaningful in the face of the events of

World War I and all that those events implied. It was no longer possible to engage in a kind of humanistic Christianity that had been common to many in Europe. He felt that neither he nor the people to whom he was preaching were finding much meat in his sermons, and in this world of uncertainty Karl Barth began to seek for more certain answers which he could preach. He decided there was a source of authoritative answers: "We took as our starting point what God Himself said and still says concerning the knowledge and reality of God by way of the self-testimony which is acceptable and comprehensible because it has been given human form in Holy Scripture."[32] What Barth seems to be saying is that the thing to do in a time when values are shaken, when meaning is gone, is to find something that you can affirm finally and absolutely, and that which Barth found to affirm finally and absolutely was God speaking of himself in Holy Scriptures. Barth thought that the Bible has the final word about God, and the Bible is that book which God himself has authenticated. He felt that nothing could be more certain than this, and on this groundwork one could build a church dogmatic.

The word that Karl Barth began to proclaim was soon heard around the world in theological circles. Barth says himself that it was as if he were groping in a darkened bell tower and had grasped hold of the bell rope, thus ringing the bell, and everyone had come running. But whatever the figure, it is certain that theology of the more classical variety began to thrive again throughout the world. People began to echo the word of Barth about the certainty of God speaking to us in the Scriptures. In Scotland this proclamation was taken up by such men as John Baillie and his brother, Donald M. Baillie. John Baillie writes, for example: "I believe in God because He confronts me with a demand that brooks no refusal. He stands at the door of my heart and knocks, He is there now, I know quite well that He is there, and I know quite well that He wants more of me than I have yet given Him. He comes to me indeed with a demand, that demand is only that I should accept a gift, the gift of salvation."[33] Notice how Baillie emphasizes the presence of God in his demand and in his gift.

This theology, because it was born in crisis, and because it pointed to the eternal crisis of man, came to be called crisis theology. It was not long before the crisis theology leaped across the Atlantic to the United States. At that time the United States was perhaps twenty-five years behind Europe in theological development, and it is somewhat surprising to discover that crisis theology took root and flowered rapidly in America. Another name given to this same theological revival is neoorthodoxy, and in America this latter is the more popular and more common word used to describe it. Although it certainly began earlier, the peak of the theological revival in the United States can be said to parallel the revival of the churches, that is, roughly 1940 to 1960. Neoorthodoxy is identified in America with several different figures, but the foremost of them is probably Reinhold Niebuhr.

The new theology made itself felt in several ways in America. In sermons, for example, it took the form of assuring man that God was seeking to encounter him, that man had not been left on his own, but that God was still actively working with this world. Furthermore, emphasis was placed upon the sinful nature of man rather than on the unlimited possibilities for man. Most notable of all was the attention given to creedal statements and their elaboration. There was a return to the historic creedal statements of the church, to what had been found most

certain and most valuable in its experience. The following
is a quotation from one of the preachers very much affected by neoorthodox theology. He writes, in a book
called *Faith and Conflict:* " The gospel claim is that something has happened, God who approaches man has encountered man who comes from God. This makes Christianity happen. And this event is man's only hope, man
who comes from God can and does meet the God who is
anxious to be known. Man the finite can encounter the
infinite. Man the limited can enter relationships with the
illimitable. I can know Other."[34] The emphasis on encounter is plain here and the same emphasis can be seen
running through much of the theology that stems from
Karl Barth and Emil Brunner.

FROM RELIGIOUS EDUCATION TO CHRISTIAN EDUCATION

The impact of the theological revival brought a sharp
critique of the general thought of liberal theology and of
religious education. In 1940, Harrison Elliott, in his work
Can Religious Education Be Christian?, sought to defend
the validity of the general tenets of the religious education
movement, while at the same time admitting some of its
obvious weaknesses. It is clear that Elliott was a much
better theologian than he was credited to be by many (of
that day or this) who are embued with the spirit of crisis
theology. Another teacher of religious education, H.
Shelton Smith, wrote a volume, *Faith and Nurture*, that
was highly critical of the religious education movement.
His book, published in 1941, was widely acclaimed as a
great step forward for religious education, mostly because
it was under the complete dominance of crisis theology.
Viewed from the vantage point of a post-Bultmannian
knowledge of theology, however, Smith's book seems little

more than a simple repetition of Brunner's theology. Elliott, while underestimating the importance of some of the issues, did deal straightforwardly with those he raised. Smith, on the other hand, set up straw men and proceeded to knock them down with borrowed theology. Like many popular books attacking liberal theology, Smith did not deal with the strongest points of religious education and its best defenders, but attacked its obvious errors and caricatured the movement as a whole. He ignored, for example, what is perhaps the major point of Elliott's work, its insight into the sociological problems that the church faced and the need to use what he termed " the Christian ideology " as the basis for the reconstruction of personal and social life. Elliott would have the church concentrate upon the religious education of adults, for this he saw as " the strategic educational problem " of the church.[35]

Whatever the merits of Elliott and the religious education movement, sharp changes were in the offing. The magnitude of them is symbolized by the decline of the term " religious education " and its replacement by " Christian education." Smarting under the critique of Smith and others, religious education hastened to be baptized into Christian education by trying to become more theological. The shallowness of many in this field is exposed clearly here, for there was never a time when religious education was lacking in theology, as we have shown; what it lacked was a self-consciousness of the theology it espoused. In this naïveté, Christian education sought to become more theological by espousing a more popular theology, insofar as the published curriculum materials were concerned. Church school materials began to evidence the vocabulary of neoorthodoxy and Biblical theology. In 1943, Randolph Crump Miller stated the needs as follows: " A theology for Christian education is

needed. The objectives, theory, and methods of Christian
education need to be undergirded and perhaps altered by
a more self-conscious theological reconstruction. . . . At
the same time, there needs to be a facing of the problem
of relating content to method in an organic whole."[36]

In 1944, the International Council of Christian Education authorized a study committee to consider " the need
of a considered statement as to the place of theological
and other concepts in Christian education." The general
theological weakness of the group is shown both in expecting a committee to clear up a problem of this magnitude
and in the fact that this seems to be the first official recognition that such a problem existed. Like the Religious
Education Association, this group assumed that theological neutrality was a possibility. James Smart's summary
comments on the report of the appointed committee seem
quite correct: " One must say frankly that it is not a book
that is likely to spark a theological revolution in the field
of Christian education. . . . It must be recognized that
from the very first page the report tends to slur over both
the issues that have created such sharp conflicts in this
field in the past and the questions on which men are
divided today. One gets the impression that everything
always has been, and still is, remarkably peaceful in this
area of the Church's life."[37]

After the report of the committee of the International
Council, a few new books appeared in the field of Christian education trying to be, or at least to sound, more
theological. The best of the day was perhaps Miller's
Clue to Christian Education, which first appeared in 1950.
Miller correctly assessed the task as follows: " Educators
must become theologians, and the theologians must become educators and the writers of lesson materials must
be grounded thoroughly in both educational theory and

theological method."[38] Miller did not realize, or at any rate did not indicate, the magnitude of the task of becoming a theologian. It is not a matter of simply mastering an acceptable theological system which can then be inserted under the educational program of the church. The problem was never that religious education had lacked a theology, but that the movement actually had several theologies and was hardly aware of any of them. It seems a bit strange also that Miller, having insisted on the importance of theology as the basis for educational method, makes it appear that any theology can serve as the basis for a system of education that will profit by his method. " The reader does not have to subscribe to the theological tenets of this writer in order to gain insight into this educational philosophy."[39] It is simply not enough and is somewhat misleading to say that " the degree to which a theology is consistent with experience and relevant to daily living determines the standard of educational effectiveness in its leading of children and adults into the Christian way."[40] We must ask with whose experience is theology to be consistent? To what kind of daily life is theology to be relevant? Miller is not ignorant of such questions, but he does not indicate for us what his answers are, nor how he arrived at them.

During the next decade and more since the writing of Miller's book mentioned above, there has been little theological effort of an original or creative nature in the field of Christian education. Lewis Sherrill, in his book *The Gift of Power*, has done the most creative work to date. This work showed great insight into the predicament of man, but saw it perhaps more in psychological than in theological perspective. Much writing in the field has come under the sway of Biblical theology or Barthian theology, but shows no evidence of having mastered it so as to be originally critical or constructive. The work for which Miller called has yet to be done. These latter remarks lead us back to the course of the theological revival in America, for as we shall see, the time is very ripe for some creative theological work.

What Has Happened to Neoorthodoxy?

Looking at the American scene, we see clearly that thousands followed gladly after the theology we have loosely termed neoorthodoxy. It seemed to have the certainty and the kind of answers that were necessary in a world of repeated cataclysms. This success, however, has not been unalloyed; some of the foremost leaders have themselves begun to raise serious questions, and it is of some note that Karl Barth and Reinhold Niebuhr hold quite differing theological views and sometimes engage in something approximating name-calling.

Neoorthodoxy eventually came to seem, to a great many who had gladly heard its promises of encounter with God, something like a false pregnancy. There was a feeling of great promise and evidence that something should be forthcoming, there should be a real fruition from this theology, but at last the agony was over, the creeds had been explored, evaluated, fought about, even thought about, but nothing had resulted. Man was still the same old man. Some of the followers, who had been so enthusiastic as to coin this little jingle, " Thou shalt love the Lord thy Dodd with all thy Barth and thy Niebuhr as thyself," began to lose their enthusiasm. What can we say of these who followed gladly and were disillusioned? That they misunderstood? Certainly this is one possibility. Another possibility is that they did indeed understand, but that certainty is incompatible with Christian faith, and encounter with God is not as simple and obvious as some made it sound. Still others became convinced that their participation in the theological revival had led them to self-deception and even to deceiving others. Let me quote here from a recent book called *The New Essence of Christianity*. " Those of us who are trying to make the Christian faith intelligible to ourselves and to others have probably spent too much time and too many words saying that we saw and believed what we did not truly see and believe. And we did not like the experience of having deceived ourselves even if we deceived no one else. But our reaction was no wiser for we began to spend even more time declaring what we could not accept and believe and we thus deprived ourselves of what power we had to live with the little that we did believe. We have taken too much pride in our affirmations and too much pride in the skill of our denials. Our denials are there, all right, but they are both unimportant and marks of our weakness, and ought to be interesting neither to ourselves nor to anyone else."[41] It is tragic that this kind of false affirmation is what tends to happen to many who become what might be called " professional Christians." Those who take up the role of minister, or Sunday school teacher for that matter, feel themselves driven to speak about experiences and beliefs that are not in fact their own. The temptation arises from the pressures of the heritage of the church, from opinions that are currently held by one's fellow Christians, and simply from the desire to be liked or to say those things which seem to be expected. When people come crying for answers, it is all too easy to give them an assurance that is not genuinely our own and to indicate that we believe things which in fact we do not know whether we believe or not. Untold numbers were trapped into this kind of situation by the theological revival with its failure to coordinate the testimony of Scripture and tradition with the internal testimony of the Holy Spirit.

Still another kind of experience can be illustrated by the parable written by Franz Kafka called "An Imperial Message." This parable concerns a dying king who commissions a royal messenger to deliver a message to you. The messenger is strong and brave and his royal commission gives him right-of-way over all others. Nonetheless, because the capital city, the palace grounds, and the castle itself are jammed to overflowing with people who have come to be present at the death of the king, the royal messenger cannot find his way through. And even if he does, there are countless dangers awaiting him between the royal city and you. Here Kafka dramatically ends— nevertheless, you sit at your window when evening falls and dream it to yourself. Thus it was with many people who looked at the theological revival, who read its reports, who heard the powerful proclamations from the pulpit, and were filled with great expectations. A glorious encounter with God, which seemed to be promised, was always at hand but never arriving. The word just never seemed to get *here*, no matter how loudly the pulpit proclaimed its presence. There were those others, too often professional Christians, who said they saw a star in the heavens, but when most of us went out to look, there was no star to be seen. It can be objected, of course, that what has been described was an improper understanding of crisis or neoorthodox theology. Nonetheless it is likely that what has been described fits rather well the common man's understanding. There were, Sunday after Sunday, tremendous pulpit proclamations about the power of the Word of God, but entirely too seldom were there those who wrestled diligently with the question of how the

Word of God strikes home into human existence and makes itself relevant to human life.

A third thing can be said about the theological revival, that is that it emphasized the sovereignty and majesty of God. This particular emphasis is probably related to the origin of this theological movement in a time of cataclysm and destruction of previously held earthly values and the consequent need for some source of certainty and security. Whether or not this theory is correct, the emphasis on the holiness and otherness of God is a fact. This theology was concerned to emphasize God's distinctness from the world in order to show that he was in no way caught up with the evanescence that characterizes human existence. It is unfortunate that for many this emphasis on the otherness of God simply meant that he was too far away, too different from man to have any identification for man or concern about his plight.

Perhaps this can be illustrated by quoting a portion from a play by a Scandinavian writer, Pär Lagerkvist, entitled *Let Man Live*. In the play, fourteen different historical characters relate the circumstances of their martyrdom. At last Jesus comes forward as one of the fourteen. The others have clearly blamed some part of society or another for their death. Now we quote from Jesus' speech. " But I, whom shall I accuse? I cannot accuse you, can I? No, of course I had to be sacrificed because that was precisely what was intended. And if you had not crucified me, what would have become of my life—of its significance? And I cannot accuse God, for of course he meant well when he sent me to you. He hoped that my coming would help you. If it has not helped, neither he nor I is responsible. We have both done our best."[42]

You and I don't exactly want to blame Jesus or God for our situation; we're not that naïve, but at the same time, when we're being honest at least, we must confess that Jesus' coming doesn't exactly, at the moment, seem to be entirely relevant, or maybe we just haven't seen the relevance of it. Somehow or other, as mankind today tends to look at things, this is the question that it raises about traditional Christology. So we turn our glance upon ourselves and we feel sure that we must be to blame and therefore that God blames us for the situation of the world. After all, as Jesus continues: "My father is full of reproaches against you. He judges you much more severely for he has never lived among you. Then it may seem to you that he is not qualified to understand you. That while he has never himself experienced your lot he cannot sit in judgment upon you. That he is altogether too unfamiliar with your difficulties and far too remote. Yes, he is. He is in one way a stranger in his own life, in the life he has created. And you are right in saying that he is very remote. He is far far away, he lives in an entirely different world. You might say in an altogether different universe from the one you call yours."[43] Many people under the preaching of crisis theology found that this was the essence of what they heard about God. That he was far away and the redemption that he had worked in Jesus Christ was also distant, that is, it took place in Jesus Christ for all men, but no one was explaining exactly how this had much to do with one's own human existence here and now. There was an assurance that I was identified with him and that he was identified with me and that now things were all right between me and God, and I was simply to believe this and be saved. It cannot obviously be contended that this was the pattern for all people, for it certainly was not. Nonetheless, it can be contended that this is a reasonable expression of the way many people experienced their encounter with the preaching of the theological renewal in America.

There are times when Christianity can attend, with much profit, to those who stand well outside the Christian pale, because their insights into life, in fact into theology, may be of inestimable value. The following passage taken from one who certainly considered himself outside the Christian fold appears to have something to say to the contemporary situation, although it was written a hundred years ago. It comes from Friedrich Nietzsche in the work *Thus Spake Zarathustra.*

Zarathustra lived in the solitude of the mountains from his thirtieth until his fortieth year and enjoyed the solitude, but at last his heart changed; he discovered within himself an overflowing love of man that simply had to be shared. As he began to descend from his sublime heights of solitude, he met an old anchorite whom he had also passed on his way up into the mountains. The old man asked why Zarathustra was returning to the company of man, the land of the sleepers. The answer was a confession of love. The old saint objected vigorously that man was not worth loving, only God was worth loving and he was to be worshiped best right here in solitude. When they parted, Zarathustra asked himself, " Is it possible that this old saint of the forest has not heard that *God is dead!* "

For many people living in the twentieth century, the God " out there " of traditional and crisis theology is dead. Not that many are concerned to deny his existence as did that Russian astronaut who asserted that he did not see God on his trips around the earth, but simply that there is no experience of a God " out there " for twentieth-century man. It seems probable that for many people today the preaching of crisis theology only makes more acute their sense of the absence of God, or worse yet his irrelevance. To see why this may be true, we shall turn in the next chapter to an analysis of the most acute crisis of man in modern history, the breakdown of the symbols by which he knows himself and understands himself and his life. Before we leave the present chapter, however, a few words must be said about some current images of the ministry that divorce it from personal and painful theological endeavor both in learning and in teaching.

THE UNTHEOLOGICAL MINISTRY

Much of the ministry during the past century, especially in American churches, has become increasingly removed from the actual task of theology. The statement is truer in American churches because they have moved farther in the direction of becoming carefully organized institutions of which the minister is the general director or manager; hence his work has become increasingly organizational and administrative in nature. But this is by no means the whole of the picture; there has been a general drift from theology over this long period of time. There was and is some revitalization from the impact of the theological revolution begun by Barth, but in the main the drift continues. To say "untheological ministry," as has been done here, does not mean that there is no theological position taken by the minister in his work or in his sermons, or in whatever teaching he does. Rather, it means that the position taken is one that is largely borrowed; it is a secondhand system that he himself has not really thought through as to its grounds and adequacy. There is no necessary implication of insincerity, either. The relation to theology is complex, but we may speak of several kinds of ministers as typical. These are, of course, hypothetical categories and no one man will fit any of them exactly. They do not adequately explain anybody's ministry, nor are they intended to be exhaustive, but they are helpful in grasping the nature of what is too often happening in the ministry today.

The Uneducated Evangelical

There are still a surprising number of ministers in America who have not darkened the door of a theological seminary. Such a pattern was more than common in the nineteenth century and stems from the frontier situation where ministers were desperately needed and none were available. It also stems from the coming into existence of multiple denominations in which there was no provision for measuring the qualifications of a man for the ministry except his suitability to the local congregation. In this rash mood even children under six were ordained by some frenzied groups who believed they could detect the gift of the Spirit at such a tender age. Today, the "uneducated" evangelical minister for the most part has attended college and perhaps graduated, but probably it was a small "Bible College." In these, too often, the theological training given is of a highly biased nature, mainly an indoctrination with that particular denomination's doctrinal prejudice, but no introduction even into the great heritage of the whole church down through the ages or of the writings of the great contemporary theological minds. The ministry of this person is untheological because it is based upon the assumption that he already has a full and adequate theology. Thus it does not incorporate that most important principle of the Reformation that the church is never reformed and must ever be reforming. Theology is an unending task and no one undertakes it if he thinks that it is done. Further, this person does not have the tools with which to engage in theology; his education is defective. One cannot do good theological work without coming to grips with the thought that has gone before as well as contemporary thought, and without being able intellectually and emotionally to be critical of it.

Educated Piety

The pietistic tradition that began in the eighteenth century in Germany has a large and continuing influence in
the church today and its influence is by no means restricted to those churches which are directly related to
the pietistic movement. As it commonly exists today, the
theological result of the influence of pietism is a conviction that theology is not really very important; it is prayer,
reading the Bible, and meditating on God that count. This
prayer may be an intercession with God for the supposed
needs of the world, a plea for personal faith, a confession
of sin and unworthiness, pleas for the holiness of the
church and of the congregation, and thanksgiving for all
manner of things, but it is always mainly asking God for
something or other, and usually at great length. The theological implications of that which is requested, and the
act of requesting at all, are usually not explored. The Bible
is read devotionally, and great portions may be memorized. The work of contemporary Biblical scholars, however, is not taken seriously, nor is the implication of the
Bible for the life of the daily world sought with vigor.
The meditation is not on the meaning or the implications
of God's concern for all being, but on the assurance that
is given by God's love or Jesus' shed blood. Piety does not
seek to love the world and give itself for the life of the
world, but to find security from the world and assurance
within. Educated piety may be found in any denomination, in any church large or small, city or rural. It may
continue a lifetime and grow ever more saccharine, or it
may turn bitter (though usually only at the unconscious
level) because God has not brought about the expected
fulfillment. Certainly, a theological position is implicit
here, but it is not thought out or expressed. There is no

grappling with theology because theology is believed to be irrelevant. When educated piety uses the word "theology," it usually means one of the nineteenth-century renditions of a classical system, for example, someone's systematic theology that is really no more than a rehash of Calvin and not nearly as good. Its genuine theological diet today is the endless series of "religious novels" and daily devotional works, or devotional Bible study materials, or worst of all, the "how to practice the Christian life" books, that is, how to get through life without having to live it.

The Educated Orthodox

Ministers of this type are mostly found within the denominations that stress their own theological creeds, the confessional churches. Their theology is composed of the confessional statements and catechisms of their denomination, whether written in the sixteenth or nineteenth century. Having once learned a theological system, they are convinced that they now have the answers, and besides, it was so much trouble to learn one system that they are never going to learn enough about another to compare them. The system may be incorporated in the liturgical practices of the church rather than in a creedal statement, but the attitude is the same. One gets the feeling from these people that if the creed is really believed, or the liturgy really practiced by the whole church for just one day, then the Kingdom of God will appear. Alteration is neither desirable nor possible. When these men teach their people, it is "what Presbyterians believe" or "what Lutherans believe" or "what Episcopalians believe," and their teaching does not bother to ask what a Christian can or might believe or what it might have to do with life today. The educated orthodox rejects and usually does not read contemporary theology because it has departed from the "faith once delivered to the saints," and does not theologize because it feels no need to do so. At the same time, it does not usually live by the theology that it professes and cannot explicate the theology that it actually lives by. Theology for orthodoxy is a system to be believed intellectually only; it does not need and mostly does not have any clear connection with the moment-to-moment decisions of daily life. In its functional theology it may not be significantly different from either of the first two types we have discussed, all three of which are basically living on the assumption that what Christianity really says is " be good and be saved "—being good meaning to believe the right doctrines and do the right things, and being saved meaning getting to go to heaven when you die and there being proved to have been on the right side all along.

The Divine Promoter

Ministers who possess intellectually the theological bent of any of the above three types may have a functional theology that is basically that of American business. Their goal is the growth of the institution called the church, and growth is measured in the simplest terms available: numbers, budget, and buildings, not to mention salary and staff. Originally their sincerity may be great, but with the functioning theology that they hold in an unexamined way, it is unlikely that they will escape becoming monument builders. Suburban America today is dotted with great stone monuments to the ambition of young vigorous ministers who saw no difference between the church and the institution and psychologically could not separate themselves from the institution. Precisely because these men would be successful in American business, they are successful in the church. They move from small to big, from poor to rich, from low to high in the hierarchy. Because they lack real theological understanding they can be the kind of religious leaders that many in their congregations demand. Their sermons are models of ambiguous clichés that can be interpreted as desired. On national occasions they properly support America with God, and on religious occasions support God with America. At funerals they subtly blend poignancy and sentimentalism into romantic illusion. Physically and sartorially they are models of taste and refinement combined with that wholesome all-American-boy look. They are finely tuned intellectually to capture the latest trends in popular thought on every superficial matter and every superficial thought about profound matters, with which to make their sermons definitely contemporary and empty. Deceiving everyone, but most of all themselves, they lead the church ever onward to greater heights of institutional success and Christian suicide. It simply would never occur to them to theologize; that is not their job, and besides, it has been done, and more yet, what does that have to do with the work of the local church?

It should be made clear here that no distinction is made between the category of minister and that of Christian educator. So far as this analysis above is concerned, the ministry includes all those who call themselves Christian educators, as well as those who are ministers of preaching, pastoral counseling, or whatever. More yet, it is neither intended nor implied that all ministers fall into any one nor any combination of these types. Many, many ministers are faithful and diligent in theological study and teaching. Nonetheless, these types are prevalent and very powerful images for the American minister and each in its own way precludes the kind of earnest theological endeavor that we shall try to show is essential to a vital life for the church in the twentieth century.

Chapter III

Western Civilization in Crisis:
The Breakdown of Symbols

MAN, THE SYMBOL USER

IT HAS BECOME increasingly apparent that it is appropriate to speak of a consensus in the fields of psychology, philosophy, and theology to the effect that man understands himself and his world by symbols. It is not too much to say that man finds meaning to his life or understands the meaning of his life only as he evaluates it by means of symbolic constructions. Some three decades ago the social philosopher George Herbert Mead showed, in his writings, that it was necessary for an individual to be able to use symbols before a self could exist. More yet, he indicated that it was necessary for symbols to have come into existence before man as an organism could develop a self. Mead spoke primarily of language symbols and indicated that in the history of the race it was necessary for their use to have been developed before one could know himself to be a self. Thus the whole construction of the self, in Mead's viewpoint, arises from the manipulation of verbal symbols.[44] Writing from quite a different viewpoint, Reinhold Niebuhr in *The Self and the Dramas of History* speaks of man's ability to transcend himself. Niebuhr means man's ability to step aside and look at himself more or less objectively or at least to look at himself, while being a self at the same time, by talking about himself and carrying on a conversation within himself. This view would seem clearly to imply the necessity of symbolic structures of a language nature. Still other scholars, writing from differing viewpoints, such as Susanne K. Langer, Charles W. Morris, or Rollo May, deal with the problem of man as a symbol user and indicate the centrality of the use of symbols to the nature of the self. All these thinkers, and many besides, have indicated in their writings that a man simply would not be what he is were he not a symbol-using creature. Without the use of language, the consensus seems to be, man simply would not be man.

Now we must explore more fully what we mean by saying that man understands who and what he is and that he is a self only by the use of symbols. We shall use the term "symbol" here in a very general sense to denote anything that can convey meaning. Thus, in its broad sense, a symbol might be any sort of object or drawing or sound that could convey meaning, that is, which could represent something else. Ordinarily that something else represented would not need to be present, but could very well be. Obviously this is a nontechnical usage of the word "symbol," but for the purposes of this discussion it is adequate. A symbol can take on almost any form, as indicated; it could be a word, a gesture, a shrug of the shoulders, an expression of the face, for all these are common symbols. A symbol can also be more complex, combining several of the former. It is generally agreed now that thinking goes on in the human mind at levels other than the simple manipulation of words in small groups. Exactly how this process proceeds is not known.

Some of the complex symbols can suggest to one a whole aspect of life, a way of thinking about life. Consider sex symbols. These latter are used widely by Madison Avenue today because they suggest certain things about life. These symbols put across a kind of feeling or emotion that the advertiser wishes to connect with the particular product he is promoting. Thus we see a very attractive young couple, obviously in a romantic situation; perhaps, to carry it a step farther, attired in bathing suits, yet looking very wholesome, clearly engaged in witty conversation and each smoking a cigarette. The entire scene points toward a highly romanticized portion of life and one that is heavily laden with the emotion of sex, and this emotion is then attached to the activity of smoking. One is expected to associate smoking this particular brand with romance and all that it implies. Thus it is that a complex symbol can suggest a whole aspect of life.

Another such complex symbol is a flag. Take the American flag; looked at nonsymbolically, it is composed of a number of pieces of cloth in three colors. For any who know America, however, and much more for those who are patriotically inclined, the United States flag is certainly much more than a multicolored piece of cloth. Many people find their heartbeat elevated simply by seeing a flag flying in the breeze, and most Americans are stirred, at least a bit, by a military parade. These reactions exist because a flag symbolizes life in a certain context; because it means being an American. Those whose faith, as we will later define that term in this book, is vested partially or wholly in the United States would find the flag symbolizing that which makes life meaningful for them, that which sums up the worthwhileness of their existence, or to which they point as the source of meaning for them. In the same fashion, for many Christians, God is the symbol that performs this function. It is certainly not just the flag, nor is it just the word " God," that either is concerned about. It is, rather, what these bring forth in the mind, the conception that these two symbols represent. The cross is a symbol of this kind also. The cross brings into the mind of the individual who sees it or who thinks it a whole conception of life, a whole understanding of life.

A further fact that should be noted about these more complex symbols is that they arise out of living situations which are meaningful to the people who use the symbols. Symbols of this kind are not invented, that is to say, one does not suddenly decide that he needs a symbol, sit down, and create one. One does not suddenly draw two intersecting lines on a piece of paper and infuse it with all the meaning of the cross. Symbols of the type at hand come into existence in a historical context. Their meaning is derived from that historical context. In a certain sense man does create symbols, because he selects them from the storehouse of history and it is man's usage that gradually elevates a symbol from obscurity to awareness. Perhaps, for the sake of simplicity, it is best to say that symbols are accidental products of man's history.

Meaning and Symbols

We now turn to consider how it is that man reflects upon the meaning of his life by virtue of symbols, and how he sees that meaning only in relation to these symbolized structures. Without symbolic structures man would find life meaningless. The psychoanalyst has pointed out that symbols can sum up the meaning of one's life or can present to him the problem that is dominating his life. For example, if one follows, more or less, the significance of dreams according to the Freudian and neo-Freudian line, one would say that a person who had a recurring dream with the same basic theme was expressing to himself a certain kind of problem in his life. If one then could discover the meaning of the symbolization used, he could uncover the problem that was plaguing this particular person. An example of a dream that occurs to many people frequently or recurrently is one that depicts unpreparedness. Perhaps, in the dream, one finds himself simply unable to get ready for a school examination. While he is dressing, the buttons do not button on his clothes, but break off instead, or his shoes have disappeared, or the car won't start, or the bus simply does not arrive, or he arrives at school to discover that he has left pencil and paper behind, or that he has arrived an hour late for the examination, and so on and on. The exact interpretation of a particular dream would of course depend upon an individual life, but in general one could say that this kind of dream expresses a pervading sense of inadequacy coupled with the fear of being exposed, that is, of having his inadequacy pulled out and shown to be what it is. Symbols such as the above may be exceedingly complex and very obscure, and although the interpretation of dreams is far from being a science, nonetheless it is quite suggestive of the way we use symbolic structures to depict our life situation to ourselves.

Man is necessarily and involuntarily concerned about his own existence, about his life situation. Man always reacts to life with some " feeling," even if it is a feeling of passivity, or indifference, for even these latter are " feelings." This " feeling reaction " cannot be reduced by any means to a simple pain-pleasure dimension. Many psychological studies are greatly weakened by reductionism, or oversimplification of the nature of man, making him little more than a complicated mechanical animal responding mainly to external stimuli as these are experienced in the pain-pleasure realm. The feeling with which man reacts to life, and react he must, has quite a different character. It is perhaps best at this point simply to say that it has the character of meaning, that is, of good or evil, right or wrong, of desirable or undesirable, of boring or exciting, of anxiety or well-being, and so on. Such a list could be made almost endlessly of the various " feeling reactions " that man can have to life and it is fairly clear that man's needs cannot be reduced to self-preservation, race-preservation, nor to tension-reduction needs, such as we find particularly in some older psychological writings. It is clear that these latter are not adequate for explaining man's behavior, and in particular they are inadequate to explain his symbolic behavior. Indeed, much of man's symbolic behavior, as can be seen from a study of primitive religions, has a negative survival value so far as survival in this world is concerned. Even the need to preserve the race would seem to be denied under the guidance of certain primitive religious symbolism. The concepts of survival and tension reduction are very useful in understanding certain portions of man's behavior. However, they are not adequate concepts for the total scope of man's behavior and this is particularly true of his symbolic behavior.

Man's concern over his life, from which arises his " feeling reaction " to life, is not adequately explained by these more simplified concepts. Man's necessary concern about his own existence is based upon his unique quality of temporality. Man does not live simply in a hairline present. Rather, he lives his life in three dimensions: the past, the present, and the future. These three constitute the dimension of temporality. Further, man has attitudes that arise out of all three of these and that are directed toward all three. There is a certain interrelationship in these three ecstasies of time, so that man cannot be seen as simply being here and now in this given moment. To understand man, one must look at him in the wholeness of his temporal situation. And that wholeness includes his past, the interpretations of it and attitudes toward it, the way he is thinking about the present, and reacting to it, and his anticipations of the future.

This quality of temporality is based upon man's character as a symbol maker and user. The mind arises only with the ability to use symbols, and the ability to relate to time in this threefold way arises only through the use of symbols. It is frequently noted that animals do not worry about dying. They do have instincts for avoiding dangerous situations, but they do not worry about death itself. We may well ask why this is so. Animals do not worry about death because they do not anticipate the future, and they do not anticipate the future because such a thing as the future is not possible without the highly developed use of symbols. A symbol enables one to separate oneself from the immediate present and to adventure both into the future and into the past. An animal learns, but does not learn mainly by the apprehension of symbols, and thus is fairly adequately understood by the model of a stimulus-response mechanism. With man it is not so. Man utilizes symbols to present to himself patterns that might in the future come into existence or that he would like to bring into existence. The basic resources for the construction of these patterns lie in man's history, but he is free to make unique combinations of these symbolic structures; indeed, his very freedom stems from this. Thus, the genuinely novel can come into existence. An animal simply cannot and does not engage in this kind of activity, animal reactions being mainly in the form of instincts, that is, innate or inborn traits of behavior which can be modified by conditioning, as in a stimulus-response mechanism. Thus, animal learning is somewhat different from human learning and is, so far as we can tell, fairly adequately understood on the basis of trial-and-error-type learning. Man learns, or learns to learn, in a different way, by projecting himself into the future and by reflecting upon the events of the past. Man reacts to life, then, with feeling, and the kind of feeling depends upon the way in which he symbolizes the meaning of his life. The feeling depends upon the symbolic structure that he holds up before him in order to evaluate himself. The nature of these symbolic structures will be considered further a little later on.

Man's Loss of Confidence in His Symbols

A very strange thing has happened in our century, and while it has probably happened before, it is certainly at an unusually high level of consciousness in our day. Certainly this phenomenon is more widespread than it appears to have been in previous history. That strange thing is that man has lost confidence in his symbols. A similar kind of pattern can be seen in the history of more primitive societies as they experienced the impact of the so-called higher civilizations. A very tragic story was written in American history when the white man moved in and imposed his symbolic structures upon the Indian culture, thereby destroying or weakening the symbols by which the Indians lived. When the symbolic realities that formerly gave meaning were taken away from the Indian, his reason to live evaporated and, unless he was willing to become like a white man, his sense of personal value degenerated rapidly. A similar kind of thing is occurring to Western civilization.

The symbols that formerly had great power to move men are weak, or powerless, or even dead. Consider the symbols father and mother: in the late Victorian era children were expected to show a deference for father and mother amounting almost to reverence, and were expected to regard themselves as somewhat inferior creatures. Instant obedience was expected and required of these children. It is clear that these patterns have changed. This is not to say that things were right then and that they are wrong now, but is given as evidence of the loss of meaning of certain symbols. To the late Victorian child the word "father" or "mother" had a great deal more power to move him than it does most of us. If one reads over some of the sermons of the first one or two decades of this century, one will observe that father and mother were apparently very moving figures to whom one would give obedience or deference and for whom one might be willing to give up his life. Mother's Day was a very important event in our land only some quarter of a century ago, rather than simply being an occasion on which one is expected to give his mother a present. Today it is difficult to find a young person who is moved by the phrase "the sacredness of motherhood," that is, unless he is moved to laughter. The glory and the glamour have departed from fatherhood and motherhood.

Another symbol that has become greatly weakened is the United States flag. If we consider some of the events and the songs surrounding World War I, it is obvious that the flag had a power then to move people which it no longer has now. Even the rugged face of Uncle Sam staring at one from the enlistment poster was a powerful symbol in those days. But can you imagine one rushing to enlist now because a gaunt, bearded figure clothed in a star-studded top hat pointed his finger and said, Uncle Sam needs you? Yet millions were apparently willing to go and save the world for democracy in the name and figure of Uncle Sam not more than fifty years ago. Flag Day, once observed rigorously throughout the United States, with the flag flying in front of every house, now passes with little notice.

The same kind of thing has happened with the symbol God; it too has lost its power to move people. In time gone by there was some kind of universal reverence or at least fear of God. The universality of this fear or reverence is seen easily in the judicial system in the required oath for witnesses. To be sworn in as a witness, one takes an oath before God and places his hand on the Bible and thereby certifies his intention of telling the truth. Can it be imagined, however, that such an oath has a very great effect on whether or not the average witness will tell the truth? It is apparent that such an oath was quite effective once upon a time; having sworn before God that he would testify truthfully, one was afraid not to. Today, doubtless some people would be afraid of God, but for the most part, the only fear involved relates to the penalty for perjury. The symbol God has lost its power.

Still another symbol that has lost its power to move people is the symbol success. Success was a powerful motivating symbol in the United States scarcely fifteen years ago, but an examination of events of the past decade indicates that success is beginning to lose its power. People are certainly less interested in ostentatious success than they were at the close of World War II, and it seems that social acceptance has largely taken the place of success. What seems important now is having acceptance from one's fellowman, or at least having his assurance that one is a part of the general social order and that things are really all right, that the world is a safe place in which to live.

Even love has lost its power as a symbol. The sex

symbols do not excite and fascinate as they did not too many years previously. Neither does love of a more inclusive nature carry a very great impact for the average life. People are admonished to love, told that this is necessary for satisfactory life, advised to give of themselves and to receive, but for the most part this advice is received very nonchalantly.

Many people have experienced and taken note of this breakdown in symbols. One such is the writer Ernest Hemingway, who notes the following in his book *A Farewell to Arms:* " I was always embarrassed by the words sacred, glorious, and sacrifice and the expression ' in vain.' We had heard them, sometimes in the rain almost out of earshot so that only the shouted words came through, and had read them, on proclamations, now for a long time, and I had seen nothing sacred, and the things that were glorious had no glory and the sacrifices were like the stockyards at Chicago if nothing was done with the meat except to bury it. There were many words that you could not stand to hear and finally only the names of places had dignity. Certain numbers were the same way and certain dates and these and the names of places were all you could say and have them mean anything. Abstract words such as glory, honor, courage, or hallow were obscene beside the concrete names of villages, the numbers of roads, the names of rivers, the numbers of regiments, and the dates."[45]

The breakdown of symbols is not imaginative; it is a factual situation. The symbols before which we necessarily must find meaning for our existence simply have no more power for us. These symbols simply are not what they once were to our general civilization. There are certainly exceptions to this, but in general it must be said that the symbols which were live symbols, which had tremendous power to influence life and to infuse it with meaning, which expressed the very essence of the meaning of our culture not more than a quarter of a century ago, are very greatly weakened or indeed perhaps totally dead.

Many factors are involved in this breakdown of symbols, but of these, three seem most important in rendering our symbols powerless. One is the reduction of the size and mystery of the world by virtue of the improved techniques of transportation and communication. This increased interrelationship has exposed us to other times, places, civilizations, cultures, societies and peoples, values and religions. This interrelationship has forced upon us the comparative study of other cultures. This process has added to the devaluation of our own culture by showing the relative nature of our own values. We can no longer regard our value system as the only possible one. In certain respects, for example, even primitive cultures can seem superior to our vaunted Greco-Roman West with its Judeo-Christian religion. For example, some psychologists and anthropologists believe that the child-rearing practices of the Peloponnesian peoples are superior to ours in that they produce many fewer neuroses. Even such a simple fact may have great implications as a person asks himself, Why do we practice child rearing as we do? The answer is simply, It is a value held in our culture. Ah, but why do we hold this value? There is usually no quick or secure answer to this latter question, and thus without it, doubt arises; we are no longer so sure that we believe what we believe. Further, we know today of many other civilizations beside ours that have grown, flourished, and apparently had some satisfactory kind of life completely apart from Christianity and from our classical or scientific heritage. Once, we could believe that Christianity was necessary for high civilization, but that is no longer believable. Once, we could believe that only a culture that was built upon the Greek and Roman heritage of scientific thinking and law could be a great and satisfactory civilization, but we no longer can believe this, for we know of these others which have operated without it. The comparative study of other cultures has begun to break down our naïve satisfaction with our own and our assurance about its God-given nature.

Secondly, the acids of the scientific world view have played their part in the weakening of our symbols. To a large extent, the coming of science has destroyed the world view upon which our civilization was constructed. That view was basically mythological. The major structures of Western civilization were from the outset held within a framework of mythological symbols. Because modern man no longer believes myths of the Biblical type and in fact seldom understands their original meaning, he is cut off from the rootage of his own civilization. The scientific world view, built into modern man by his vaunted educational system, is fundamentally incompatible with the mythological world view incorporated in the writings of the Jewish and Christian religions. As we shall see later, what the myths actually mean is not at all destroyed by the scientific world view, but it is no longer possible for man to live in a mythological world. Or to put it differently, it is no longer possible for man to " think his world " in mythological terms.

Thirdly, the events of the twentieth century have been profoundly destructive of our symbols. These events reflect, primarily, simply the climax of the industrial revolution, its increasingly rapid pace, the vast and pervading changes in patterns of living, so that we are almost totally divorced from the cultural situation that we had only ten or fifteen decades ago. World War I can be said to mark the end of faith in man. As we have noted earlier, the naïve optimism of the late nineteenth and the early twentieth century came to an end with World War I. Any further belief in the inherent goodness of man was nothing more than a hangover from this earlier period and was doomed to death. World War II ended our faith in nations; after this we no longer believed that man's social structures could be considered sacred. And the events that have transpired since that time have added to this weakening. Few Americans, for example, are convinced that the " American Way of Life " is the only " right way of life," and that our nation is the only " right kind of nation " in the world. Most Americans, at least those of reasonable intellect, would agree that it is as probable that Western Europe will set the pattern of progress in government as it is that the U.S. will. Finally, the twentieth century has brought us an almost unbelievable amount of comfort, by previous standards, freedom from being wage slaves, but all this has not brought any pervading sense of well-being or happiness. We are not satisfied with the situation as it is; few are convinced that it is radically right and good and meaningful; instead, the meaning of life has been called into question more seriously than ever before. Running through the class structure almost from top to bottom is a lack of assurance, a serious questioning about the meaning of life, not always verbal or even conscious, but real enough. We suspect, now, that life isn't all about making money, nor about being comfortable, nor about saving the world for democracy, so, what is it all about?

As people sense this vacuum, they begin to seek for ways and means to fill it. The first recourse is to science and technology, the means that delivered us from the old enemies, the assumption being that we can refine the processes of our social system and alleviate our difficulties.

Thus we see the fervent application of the social sciences
to business and government. Also, there is a turn to psychological tinkering with the self, the effort being to correct the errors that are inside us. These are the methods
which the scientific world view indicates are most appropriate to our plight. If a person's orientation is religious,
and he holds the scientific world view, then he takes up a
course of applying the techniques of the religious life to
himself and others, as he views the religious life. Thus it
is that we get books on the ABC's of having a better and
more successful religious life by knowing and applying its
techniques; then we can have peace, poise, power, and
personality. One can learn the techniques of prayer and
thus be equipped to get God on one's side. If a person's
orientation is secular, he might, for example, pick up a
book on sex technique, feeling sure that if he can just
master the technique, then his sexual problems will be
straightened out and things will be all right within him.
In such thinking there is little recognition of the highly
complex relationship between a man and a woman which
determines whether the sexual union will be delightful
or detestable.

The breakdown of traditional symbols and the loss of
the mythological world view are the basic reasons for the
growing inability of the theology generated by the theological revival to penetrate American culture. The theological revival has largely refused to utilize any but Biblical
and traditional language. There has been particular resistance to any and all attempts to translate the Biblical
myths into contemporary meanings.

The first step in any constructive attack on the problems of ministry, whether pastoral or educational, is a
careful analysis of some of the central concepts of Christianity. These central concepts must be translated into

descriptive terms understandable by twentieth-century man. The following chapters will undertake this analysis in at least a preliminary way. It seems necessary first to examine the concept *faith*. Keeping in mind Calvin's admonition that the knowledge of man and the knowledge of God hang together, we shall not be afraid to begin with man. Indeed, we have little choice, for the Barthian method of beginning with God has begun to seem sterile in many respects. At the least, it needs to be supplemented by a phenomenological analysis of faith that begins with man. Next, we shall analyze man's experience of God. These chapters must then be connected with the Biblical expression, and to do so we must analyze Biblical history to see how Jesus came to be called the Christ of God. Next, we face the general question of Biblical interpretation in our day, particularly what it means to meet the Christ. Then in a final chapter we can have a look at the new man who is arising in our age, seeing him in theological perspective, and thus attempt to determine what kind of professional ministry the church needs in our day.

Chapter IV

Faith and Christian Faith

IT IS UNFORTUNATE that the word " faith " has been
so misused and abused in recent centuries that it can
scarcely be restored. The major confusion is between two
ideas: that of faith as a certain body of doctrine which is
believed and, on the other hand, that of faith as an activity
of the whole human personality. Some of the blame for
this tragic confusion must be laid upon those who stood
in the earlier centuries of the church when it became
common to speak of *The Faith;* but we have our own
blame to shoulder as fundamentalists, liberals, or high
churchmen. In any case, it is too late to hope that we may
still recover the use of the word " faith " in any pure sense,
but what we can and must do is recover the concept of
faith as a central activity of the human personality, for
this latter kind of faith is a dynamic heart of the Christian
life.

THE MEANING OF FAITH IN THE MIDDLE AGES

Let us look momentarily at the understanding that the
common man of the Middle Ages had of the nature of
faith in order that we may better understand the confusion in our own day. The period of the middle ages is
often described as an age of faith. The question that most

tortured the soul of man in that age was, How can I be saved? Man was driven to ask this question and agonize over it because that age was a time of fear and superstition, an age when God was indeed a most threatening figure and a most arbitrary one. The earth was viewed as a vale of tears and trial, and God as ever ready to condemn the soul to an eternity of torture, a literal lake of burning brimstone, and at the slightest provocation. Small wonder, indeed, that the soul of man was tormented to ask, How can I be saved?

The noteworthy things for us can be discovered by asking what was meant by that ever-present question. Behind the query seems to lie a search for an escape from the wrath of God, a quest for some way to placate God's anger so that the fires of hell can be escaped. At that time, as it still does at some times and places, the church was giving an answer to man's question in the same terms in which the question was asked. The church proclaimed that it held the keys to the Kingdom of Heaven; that it could literally open and close the gates of a literal heaven and hell. The key of salvation was faith; the church here had the right word, but, as evidenced by the way the common man grasped its teachings, it had an improper understanding of faith. Let us see then what faith meant in the life of the people. First of all, faith meant believing the church. In particular, having faith in this way was to be evidenced by obedience to the commands of the church and by orthodoxy in holding the doctrines of the church. Neither obedience nor orthodoxy was expected to include understanding; that is, a person was not expected to concern himself with why he was to do a particular act that was commanded; it was enough that he do it because it was commanded. Unquestioning obedience, especially among the monastic orders, was a mark of good faith. Nor was one expected, or allowed for that matter, to ask why or whether certain doctrines should be believed by the Christian. It was enough that they had been officially promulgated by the church; the faith of the individual was to believe them. Secondly, faith was generated by receiving grace through the sacraments of the church. In this second sense it is apparent that both faith and grace are understood in a very objective, almost substantial, sense. It is as if grace were some sort of fluid that could be injected and received into the body or soul by the reception of the sacraments and as if faith were the pressure generated thereby. It is clear that the sacraments were believed to work in an automatic, if not magic, fashion with resulting benefits for the recipient; this latter doctrine is usually referred to as an *ex opere operato* doctrine of the sacraments. The attitude of the recipient, unless the sacrament was being ridiculed, did not appear to be significant. Thirdly, faith meant certain concrete acts of good works or worship. These acts were not results of faith but acts of faith; the difference is subtle, but important. The latter is again an objective act of obedience done because it is commanded and done usually, though perhaps subtly, to win God's favor or avoid his displeasure. Thus the church taught that it was an act of faith to venerate the relics held by the church, and that it in some way enhanced one's favor with God. Likewise, some deeds or acts of penance prescribed by the church were important in improving one's standing with God. These concrete acts or good works, in the same fashion as the receipt of the sacraments, were presumed to increase one's supply of grace and heighten one's faith.

What we are concerned to note in each case presented here is the treatment of faith as purely impersonal objective phenomena. The relationship to God that is repre-

sented by this understanding of faith is a purely impersonal one. It can be handled by an intermediary, the
church, and demands only certain prescribed and physical
acts. It is like dealing with a judge through your lawyer
or being married by proxy: one need not have his heart
in it, but need only fulfill the legal requirements. Assent
and ritual were presumed to be the essence of faith; it
was an objective and impersonal relationship to God. The
fear of hell and purgatory replaced the words of John 3:16,
" For God so loved the world," in the hearts of the people.
Obedience had replaced the Spirit in the lives of the
people. The objective, calculating, legalistic, impersonal,
had replaced the personal, I-Thou, Grace-ful, and spontaneous in their understanding of faith.

CONTEMPORARY CONFUSION ABOUT FAITH

It was suggested earlier that there is contemporary confusion as to the meaning of faith, and now we must de-
lineate some of these current confusions. The basic error
in each mistaken concept of faith is the locating of faith
in some single aspect or area of personality. This error
both assumes that the human personality can be so divided
and that faith is something which affects only one such
portion. The first incorrect idea we shall survey is the
common notion that faith means believing the right things,
giving intellectual assent to the orthodox doctrines, especially if this means believing things for which there is
small factual evidence and which seem, from a scientific
point of view at least, to be difficult to believe. This assent
is all the more credit to the believer because it requires a
certain *sacrificium intellectus*. It should be noted, however, that the fallacy involved has nothing to do with the
amount or the quality of evidence available for or against

the belief, for the fallacy is that of confusing intellectual assent with faith. It is this confusion which makes the person who holds this position prone to feel that he is especially religious and righteous when he stoutly defends certain disputed doctrines or upholds rigidly the literal interpretations of the Bible: such as a strict seven-day period for the creation of the world, or a real live fish that swallowed a real live Jonah. The word "orthodoxy" means holding the right doctrines, i.e., believing what the authorities tell you are the right things to believe. Replacing faith with orthodoxy is a real temptation to all of us because it brings such a feeling of security and escape from the terrifying responsibility of having to decide for ourselves what is correct, and, after all, we tell ourselves, that is what the experts are there for, that is what they are trained and paid to do. In actuality, orthodoxy is an attempt to be secure, to play it safe; it is, in this way, irresponsibility, and means putting one's trust in the visible authorities or turning one's life over to them, rather than bearing the burden of decision.

There is a twofold fallacy involved in holding any such notion of faith as that above. First of all, it makes our faith into an intellectual or pseudointellectual act; it turns faith into a kind of knowledge. The center of faith for a person who has this understanding is the mind, or, in the Freudian terms, the ego. It must be maintained against this view that faith is not knowledge believed on the basis of trust in the authority by which something is proclaimed, whether it be church, priest, or book. Nor is faith knowledge, in the objective sense. That kind of knowledge is the proper area of science, history, and other academic disciplines and whereas faith will involve some of these, it cannot be equated in any sense with belief in the knowledge which they produce or refute. Most of the quarrels between theology and science can be directly traced to the failure to make this very important distinction. We must not make the mistake, however, of rejecting the intellectual locus entirely, for as we shall presently see, faith includes the intellect, but our point is that faith is never merely intellectual and to make it so is to court a new gnosticism. Saving faith is not some kind of intellectual knowledge or act. Unless what one believes by his mind is believed by the rest of his personality, it does not have the character of faith, but merely assent.

The second fallacy involved in holding an intellectual notion of faith is hinted at above in the suggestion that a person holding this notion usually feels that God is in his debt or at least in some special fashion that he is on God's side. Against any such convictions, the position must be held that no one receives any credit for believing in any particular doctrine (or denying some particular doctrine, for that matter), even believing in the existence of God, as the New Testament so well points out (cf. James 2:19). Belief (faith) that is limited to the intellectual sphere is not sufficient because it does not make a real difference in one's life. One may be firmly convinced that Mt. Everest is 28,000 and some-odd feet high, but for an earthbound resident of the United States, that belief can hardly be of much consequence to one's life. In like fashion it is of little consequence that one affirm a literal seven-day creation, or any other particular doctrine, if it means only an intellectual affirmation. More important yet for our second fallacy is the fact that, however correct one's doctrine may be or however firmly one believes it, neither gives the believer a claim upon God. There are no bargains to be struck with God, no credits to be claimed from him, no way to place him in one's debt, for the fact is that " none is righteous, no not one; no one understands, no one seeks for God" (Rom. 3:10–11). New life, salvation, must and does come purely as an act of grace; it is God's gift, not something that can be earned or merited. At the same time, it is here maintained stoutly that there is all the difference in the world between the faithful and the faithless. Our point is, however, that this difference does not give the faithful any claim upon God such as the creditor has upon the debtor; both faithful and faithless are beloved equally. Does not Jesus say that God "makes his sun rise on the evil and on the good, and sends the rain on the just and the unjust" (Matt. 5:45)? Clearly then, faith does not represent a change in God's attitude, nor elevate the faithful in his sight. We must look elsewhere for the significance of this difference.

The second incorrect notion of faith that we shall survey is the common idea that faith is, like romantic love, mainly an affair of the emotions. A few generations ago, one could have pointed out a glaring example of this fallacy in the revivalist sects. William James, in his delightful work *Varieties of Religious Experience,* catalogs numerous examples of the weird phenomena among these people. Today, there are few living examples of the revivalist sect, but there is no lack of such an understanding of faith; we have merely changed our way of expressing emotion. There are still those who expect a great emotional upheaval at conversion, though seldom is it expected that this will result in the physical symptoms formerly exhibited. There is certainly no dearth of church groups that make every church service a pulpit-pounding emotional jag. We are all acquainted with the excesses of Aimee Semple McPherson and more lately of Father Divine, and others.

There are more subtle forms of this basic misunderstanding of faith as well. There is the person who says he goes to church because he likes the feeling he gets as a result, a sense of uplift and release, a sense of duty fulfilled, or just being good. Then there is the more aesthetic-minded individual who feels closer to God among the stained-glass windows, drinking in the mellow tones of the organ and the choir. Church worship and architecture can easily be spiritual narcotics that give an emotional sense of well-being that is totally unrelated to faith.

Certainly genuine faith includes emotion. The error we wish to identify here, however, is that which understands faith as being wholly or mainly of an emotional nature. It is thus gravely to be doubted that a conversion to Christian faith either can or should be sought by emotional routes such as are practiced by most mass evangelists. It is no doubt true that there are many routes open to the human soul, but to use any one virtually to the exclusion of others is to incur a considerable danger that the person will thereby misunderstand the nature of genuine faith. This position must be maintained equally convincingly against the exponents of the liturgical movement who are frequently as confused as the mass evangelist as to the true nature of faith, although their error may be either that of making faith emotional or that of making it orthodox in the sense of right ritual. God's favor is not won by sincere emotions or profound emotions, whether or not associated with right ritual and right belief. God's favor, as we have indicated above, is not won at all; it is strictly and purely a gift.

The major fallacy involved in understanding faith as something located among the emotions is that it misunderstands the nature of man and his relationship to God. It has been made increasingly clear by contemporary psychology and psychiatry that the personality of man has, in some fashion or another, a unitary nature. The now quite outmoded faculty psychology, which conceived of man having various faculties such as reasoning and emotion, simply cannot be considered as a live option. We cannot, therefore, in the realm of religion, assign faith to some faculty or other. However we understand human personality, we must recognize it as a unitary phenomenon. Thus faith cannot be reduced in any sense to an emotional phenomenon only; it must be understood as relating to the human personality.

Likewise, the position that faith is located among the emotions misunderstands the relationship between God and man. As we have illustrated above, this error may be that of expecting "orthodox" emotion to evidence a genuine conversion, or it may simply fail to understand that faith claims the whole of a person and not merely a romantic emotional response. This latter error may be fairly compared with the fact that people commonly confuse sexual excitement and attraction with love. In both cases, it is a romantic error and subject to the usual delusions and weaknesses of romanticism, not the least of which is that it cannot generate any "staying power" when the going is rough. If attendance at worship fails to elicit an appropriate emotional response, one begins to think that faith has died or that God has gone away. If one's good deeds become painful instead of pleasurable, one is convinced that God is failing to keep his promises. Thus, if being a Christian seems to bring only hardships, rebuke, and disappointment, then the whole project goes aground, sabotaged by false expectation. Clearly, faith can never be identified with any given emotional response, nor can faith demand from one's relationship to God any particular emotion as a guarantee or a reward.

A third misunderstanding of faith that we will consider briefly is that of making faith into moral obedience. This misunderstanding reduces faith to morality and makes

Christianity a moralism. In its intellectual phase, this misunderstanding is exemplified by the scribal error, the
worshiping of the law, "His delight is in the law of the
Lord, and on his law he meditates day and night"
(Ps. 1:2). In its activist phase, this misunderstanding is
exemplified by the Pharisaic error, the worshiping of
obedience to the law, "Lead me in the path of thy com-
mandments, for I delight in it" (Ps. 119:35).

By and large, in the contemporary scene, these two
phases of moralism are seen together, and they appear
both in the old liberal or modernist context as well as in
fundamentalist and orthodox groups. It is the confusion
of understanding faith as moral obedience that leads to
the legalism of the fundamentalist groups, who seem to
specialize in negativistic rules, and believe that by ab-
staining from almost anything, one is nearer to God. In
more radical settings, this line of thought produces people
who separate themselves from their fellowmen in order
that they may not be contaminated by them. In Northern
Scotland in 1960, a wave of radical separation based on
doctrinal purity swept over the more intense wing of the
Plymouth Brethren, with a result that lifelong partner-
ships in business were severed, families were split, men
resigned from jobs and unions, hardship was rampant,
and orderly society was threatened. In less radical settings, there is noted a subtle nurturing of pride among
those who are most scrupulously obedient to the "Thou
Shalt Not" and the "Thou Shalt" of their provincial
church code. Even if one were in great agreement with
the overt actions both forbidden and enjoined, one could
not fail to realize that shattered human relations and the
subtle engendering of pride in the face of God and man
are the real evils against which Jesus campaigned so
vigorously.

In the liberal or modernist setting, the understanding of

faith as moral obedience has brought about the tragic errors of " do goodism " and has reduced Christian education to character education. In reality, these groups have severed the command to love God from the command to love one's neighbor. The tragedy here is that until one understands what it means to love God and does love God, he cannot, in fact, love his neighbor, no matter how well he knows, through character education, just what that might mean. The wide experiences of modern psychiatry bear out the contention of Christianity that man is corrupted with self-centeredness and lovelessness, if not downright hatred for his fellowman. Anna Karenina, realizing the horror of this situation in her own life, is led to exclaim, " Have we not all been put into the world for no other purpose than to hate and torment one another? "[46] Until this pattern is shattered by a Word that can turn man from his self-centered way of understanding to a God-centered way of understanding, we cannot expect the love of neighbor to be a reality; it can at best be an ideal, admired from afar, but unattainable. True Christian faith begins with this shattering of trust in self and thus alone begins the understanding of the meaning of the love of God and trust in him alone.

In summary then, it is to be said that faith is not *believing the right doctrines,* whether due to authority or reason; it is not an *emotion* of any particular sort; and it is not *moral obedience.* Faith is not the *activity* of any one particular portion of the human personality. Faith is not a *basis for a claim* upon God. Faith includes the whole human personality as its locus; it participates in doctrinal expressions; it engenders emotions, and it is the basis of the love of neighbor. In the next section, we must examine what faith is in the positive sense.

THE NATURE OF FAITH

We have noted at some length in the preceding section the confused and mistaken notions of faith; in this section we shall try to develop positively the nature of faith as an activity of the whole human personality that evidences its presence in certain positive ways. Any attempt at a summary definition of faith will be beset with weaknesses, but a provisional definition will be helpful at this point. Faith, in the positive sense, is the organizing principle of the human personality.

It is to be noted immediately that this provisional definition is not restricted to Christian faith. It is intentionally not so restricted, because faith as a human phenomenon is not restricted to Christians, despite the fact that in the previous section we have dealt only with aberrations of faith as observed in the Christian community. In the sense, however, of the organizing principle of the human personality, faith is, and must be, a part of every human life. To be a person means to be one for whom faith is a necessity, not an option. No one lives without some organizing principle (or principles) for his personality. When we say organizational principle we do not necessarily mean an idea or system of ideas, but we have in mind, rather, a purely operational definition; faith is that around which human personality finds it possible to *be*. Without faith, personality does not merely degenerate, but rather, finds that life is impossible, unthinkable, unlivable. Anyone who lives, lives by faith.

A person's life is always a matter of concern to him. This does not mean merely that he has concerns or that he is at the moment worried about himself on some particular account. It is, rather, that what his life itself means is always a real question for him, though not, of course, in so many words. It is rather that his very being requires to be expressed in some particular way. *Being* cannot simply *be* in general. One has to be a particular person, not just man. And no matter how " other-directed " one is, he cannot avoid being some particular person in the most concrete possible way. Thus one's being is, with or without his choosing, an issue for him; he is concerned about himself and cannot be otherwise. To *be* is to be concerned.

Because his life is a matter of concern to him, a person desires some sort of certification or approval for the particular person he is. This may be expressed as need of approval for specific acts or thoughts, or the demand for freedom to carry out his will, or being worried that he has not done the right thing, or guilt feelings about past acts. Further, this life is lived in a world the very nature of which is best characterized by uncertainty and mystery. The history of man demonstrates his continuing lack of capacity to accept this uncertainty, this mystery, and his continual battle against it. Even the commonplace insurance policy is an evidence of man's concern about the uncertainty of the future. Man wants approval for what he is and assurance of meaning in a world of flux. Man seeks escape from his responsibility and from his evanescent situation.

To be one particular person, however, instead of another, that is, to be the particular person one is just at this moment, is an act of decision and a declaration of faith. The decision rejects other possibilities. It decides in favor of this particular possibility and thereby declares its faith in this choice. One may regret his choice, but this merely means that one no longer has faith in the choice. Faith is the basis for the choice of this possibility rather than that possibility of being.

Because one continually meets novel situations in life,

he must continually make decisions, and even habits that seemingly form a basic pattern of life may be better understood as repeated decisions. For example, does one decide once for all that he will get up at 7 A.M. on weekdays and at 8 A.M. on Sundays? Does he not in reality decide each night again, as he sets the alarm, that he will *again* rise at 7 A.M. or 8 A.M., as the case may be? There are also, of course, the inevitable unexpected occurrences that mean that one must alter his schedule; the bus changes its time of operation, or one has a golfing or fishing engagement. We noted above that faith is expressed in every decision, every commitment, and in every institution we create. Thus we must continually make and remake decisions. It is just as true that we must commit and recommit ourselves to uphold our principles in institutions. One, for example, cannot simply put one dollar or one hundred dollars in the offering plate at church and feel that his obligation to support the church has been accomplished forever. Each time the plate is offered to him he must decide anew what his commitment to the church means. Or, to give a quite different example, one must decide each day when the alarm rings whether or not he is committed to arising to carry out the purposes that were in mind when the alarm was set. If faith is truly expressed in every decision or commitment, then faith must necessarily be a thing that exists in the present only; it is, in a sense, a creature of the moment.

Faith, then, can never be viewed as an accomplished fact or permanent position. Indeed, one can scarcely speak of it as a position at all; it is that for which one decides in the present moment and upon which he stakes the meaning of his life. We seldom realize the moment-by-moment nature of faith because we wish, mostly, to escape from the enormous responsibility of actually living our own

lives. The most common, because the easiest, escape is to
become a creature of habit. We simply repeat again and
again a decision made in the past. We do not recognize it
because the decision is to do the same thing we did before
in a similar situation. In this fashion, bit by bit, we build
up great patterns of habits that run most of our lives for
us. Of course, we must recognize that the possibility of
having such automatic patterns, which we call habits, is
of tremendous value for man. For example, without it he
could not learn the muscular skills that make life possible.
If one had consciously to control every movement of every
muscle, he would get little else done. The ability to form
habits or patterns of life frees the mind for other possibilities. The fact is, however, that these patterns are ours
and not we theirs, that is, it is we who form, and reaffirm
by each repetition, a given pattern. When, however, we
choose to do so, we can easily fail to recognize our responsibility in reaffirming by repeating, and thus we feel
free of responsibility; it has hidden itself under the guise
of habit. In fact, however, we do live our own lives, no
matter how habit-ridden they may be, and we must die
our own death. No one else can do either of these things
for us, and what *we* have become, *we* are. Our decision is
what we do with it. The patterns that I reaffirm are my
expressions of faith and I must always ask why I *now*
live the way I do if I seek to know the actual object of my
faith. The object of my faith is that which motivates me
in this present moment to think and act and feel in the
ways that I do. For this reason, faith can never be viewed
as an accomplished state; it is never a thing of the past,
but only of the present.

Because faith does have the nature of an understanding
of life, it can accept ready-made answers. We shall show
the tragedy of these later. Ready-made answers are, in

fact, quite welcomed by the self, for it is concerned to have approval and assurance. A ready-made understanding always has certain "authoritative testimony"; it is popular, or scientific, or acceptable, or rational and thus we have a *rationale* for basing our being upon it. Thus it feels as if we are not any longer fully responsible for being who we are. We seem to be justified. In fact, we have simply disguised the full degree of responsibility by seeming to be able to give reasons. The fact that our *reasons* may be only folk mores does not seem to vitiate our feeling of "being right."

What, however, underlies our need to feel "right"? Why do we want the approval of a ready-made understanding? It is because we sense the potential guilt involved in grasping this particular possibility rather than that one. There is something irrevocable about such choices, for no given moment of life goes through our hands twice. Choice involves the rejection of a manifold of possibilities. Choice is a declaration, a signing on the dotted line, an unchangeable commitment. A choice is an indissoluble marriage of myself to this moment.

Considered more analytically, faith is not *primarily* in the choice of a certain possibility; it is the basis for the choice. It is only in a secondary sense that we have faith in the choice itself. Faith is primarily expressed in an *understanding of life*. Thus faith is seen to be a sort of *raison d'être*, an overall evaluation of life, albeit, a functional and not a theoretical one.

Another manner of expressing faith, besides one's decisions, that will help us to realize the meaning of having an *understanding* of life is one's reaction to life as it is given to him. Life is always received in some particular way. The evidence that it is received in some way is that we always find ourselves having some emotional tone or affective state. We may be joyful, depressed, gay, grim, or indifferent, but never are we without some emotional tone. The particular way in which we react to life in any given moment is a symptomatic reflection of our *understanding of life*. The understanding of which we speak is not, of course, necessarily a rational cognitive phenomenon. It may or may not be lifted partially to the level of conscious and verbal awareness. Further, although we may speak and think about this understanding in an abstract rational way, it cannot be lived this way. The phenomenon *understanding of life* is itself always a functional process, not merely a mental and abstract one. It cannot be abstract or equivocal because man's being is particular and unavoidable.

The Object of Faith

The faith expressed in a certain *understanding of life* is the actual basis upon which one's personality is organized. Faith, as delineated here, is the explanatory principle of any given life and it is this faith relationship which is implied when we speak of a god or an idol. It is faith which, from the human standpoint, makes the gods and the idols. A god or an idol, then, is, by this definition, anything around which human personality is organized. The purpose of the god or idol is to serve as the center, and as such, to organize the whole. Organization as we use it here means more than mere order. It means an order that has inherent meaning, that stands for something, the something being the center that infuses it with values.

We are now in a position to see that faith, as a human necessity, is expressed in a relationship to some center for the personality. This relationship has a dual quality, including both trust and loyalty.[47] As a result of the trust, one feels confident of his own life, and this sense of well-being engenders and feeds the loyalty to the object of trust. The object trusted may, quite literally, be anything imaginable; it is not limited to the objective world, but may be a principle, or ideal, hypothetical or mythological gods, nation or *ism*.

The trusted object, further, serves as the anchor point for one's sense of values, while the object itself is beyond question as to its goodness or rightness. The object is a touchstone by which other values are established. One's hierarchy of values is thus derivative in nature. It must be noted though, that there may be and often are, for any individual, multiple objects of faith, and thus multiple, even quite contrary, hierarchies of value. In this fashion, inner conflicts can and do arise, and behavior may be erratic or appear irrational. Things, events, people, and life are important or valuable according to their relationship to one's object of faith; the more significant the relationship to the faith object, the more value we accord to that person or activity, and the self is assured of worth and meaning (or even immortality) because of its relationship to the object of faith. Again let it be stressed here that the object of faith need not have any particular metaphysical status accorded to it by the person who holds this object, although it may have. In this essay it is desired to stress an operational definition of faith and the object of faith. The object is the focal point of that action, attitude, or relationship by which it becomes the organizing center for the self. It is being contended here that the best definition for a god is the same as that for the object of faith; one's god is that which actually functions as the organizing principle of the self.

Even skepticism or atheism are forms of faith and have

their god or gods according to this definition. The skeptic is, frequently, merely expressing his faith in a universe governed by irrational chance. The atheist, perhaps from a faith in causal determinism, wishes to reject the theistic understanding of the world. These are, nonetheless, expressing certain convictions about life around which their selves are organized. These expressions may be only partially conscious. In fact, few of us, it is likely, are fully aware of the nature of our objects of faith, the gods that we daily serve.

What we are concerned to make clear here is that the kind of life one actually lives is a result of his object of faith, and that the metaphysical tangles about the nature of God may be bypassed at this point of the discussion by holding to an operational definition of God as that around which one organizes his self. If this is accepted, it is clear that everyone lives by faith, and the crucial question then is, What is the object of one's faith? And what is appropriate as an object of faith? (This last question will be dealt with more fully at a later point.)

To find out what a man's object of faith is, one should ask the question, What is it that actually motivates him to live the way he does in fact live? Many a modern, for example, puts his ultimate confidence in science or the scientific method. Such a person is convinced that science has, or potentially has, the answers to all of man's problems both personal and collective. The fact is, then, that faith is expressed in every decision we make, and every commitment we express, and every institution we create. One frames his economic thinking, for example, by his convictions about the goal of life and the value of life as much or more than he does by his study of the science of economics or banking. We should note here, for fuller consideration later, that often, if not usually, a person has more than one god, that is, most people are polytheists.

One seldom encounters a person who has science as the object of his faith in every area of life. Other objects will at times replace or compete with this one, such as pleasure perhaps, or security.

Let us then summarize. Faith is a basic activity of the human being, an activity without which no man exists. Faith is, in a manner of speaking, the way one understands himself, his own existence, the why and wherefore of his life. Faith is the response of the person as a self to his whole existence, a response that is expressed in the here and now and that governs the whole of his life, ordering his personality. The object or objects of one's faith are properly called God or gods, for they receive one's supreme loyalty and are the actual motivating center for one's life. Faith is an attitude of trust and confidence that creates a touchstone for one's hierarchy of values and that infuses one's life with meaning. From one person to another, the real difference in faith is not its presence or its intensity, but the quality or nature of the object or objects of faith. The really important question about faith is, then, What is its object? or in more traditional language, What god does one worship?

CONTEMPORARY FUNCTIONING FAITHS

It may help one to grasp the nature of faith as discussed above if some contemporary functioning faiths are described briefly. Many of these can be observed in the current American scene, but only three will be described. The first might be called hedonism, because the goal or object of faith is simply being happy. Life is understood as being worthwhile and meaningful when one is happy, but somehow as being less meaningful and worthwhile if one is not happy. Happiness is usually understood in this pattern as simply having a good time, feeling well, being pleased with life because of one's environmental situation. The person who espouses this faith can be seen acting primarily so as to achieve the feeling of happiness. He buys or otherwise procures those things which produce the desired feeling: alcohol, tobacco, candy, cars, sex, prestige. These and many other things are sought and utilized for their happiness-producing quality. If a person is thoroughgoing in this faith, he will guard his health zealously, e.g., he will not eat or drink too much, for if he does, he will have a hangover or a feeling of bloated- ness with which to cope, and these are not happiness- producing. Excesses of emotion may also be avoided and a certain toughness toward life espoused, because one is less easily hurt and thus happier that way. As we shall note in the case of the other two functioning faiths to be described, Madison Avenue is well aware of the existence of this faith and appeals to it continually to achieve the sale of its products. A person is continually bombarded with the assurance that he will be happier if he switches to this brand of cigarette or antiperspirant, or that the home will be more joyous with a new stereo set, etc.

A quite different kind of faith is espoused by one who values safety and security above all else. This view con- centrates on the dangerous aspects of life and sees it robbed of meaning if there is not enough protection against these dangers, *enough* being understood as total, or all available. The meaning of life is seen in its longevity and freedom from certain threats. Such faith is perpetually occupied in planning for the future and worrying about the unforeseen eventualities that could upset the plans. Life is carried out like military strategy: today's purpose is so to act as to be free of danger tomorrow. The one who lives like this is the circumspect man, the rational man, the planner. Today is always to be sacrificed in order to secure tomorrow. When life is actually to be *lived* does not seem to be a question to this faith. The college graduate being interviewed for a job seems frequently more concerned about the retirement plan and the security of the company and his job within it than he does about the possible opportunities and challenges of the job itself. Is such an attitude not simply a manifestation of faith in security? Insurance companies, safety and civil defense planners, and banks, to mention only a few, capitalize on this kind of faith to which we are all subject at one time or another. Certainly Christian faith is not to be equated with carelessness, but Jesus did admonish us about excessive care for the future.

A third kind of faith is manifested as a compulsion to be approved, to receive acceptance from others. A person who is caught up in such a faith finds that he must seek the guidance of others on all matters. His concern is not to discover what he wants, or what is right in the sight of God, but to discover, and so far as possible, *be* what others tell him he should be. This pattern may be a subtle form of security-seeking, for when a person has the approbation of others, he feels less responsible for his own deeds if they do not achieve the desired result. If I do what others tell me is right and it fails, then it was the others who were wrong, not I. Advertising frequently plays upon our desire to be accepted and approved, assuring us that certain clothes will improve popularity and prestige. Even a certain cigarette claims to have more prestige value than others.

Faith and Christian Faith

If all these above are ways of faith, then it is clear that faith may be either Christian or not Christian. Faith in and of itself is purely a human phenomenon. The difference between one faith and another is found most easily and precisely in that toward which the faith is directed.

Non-Christian faith, whatever it may be called, is directed to something, someone, some purpose, within the creation. Christian faith, whatever it may be called, is that faith which is directed to the final power beyond the creation and forming the limits to it, the power that the Bible calls God. It is this God about whom we speak in the remainder of the discussion.

Faith in God is never an established or accomplished state; it is not a once-for-all deed or possession claimed once for all time. Faith in God is a dynamic present expression manifested in one's decision. One is always in the position of having to say, "Lord, I believe; help thou mine unbelief" (Mark 9:24, KJV). Luther recognized this character of faith in his statement that the mind of man is an idol factory. Man cannot in this moment get rid of his future idols; he can only reject the present idols that claim him. Or, one may profess faith meaningfully, while denying it at the same time. In this way one is a divided self; rival gods are at war within him. Faith in God does not eliminate doubt; its nature is trust and hope rather than certainty. But as trust and hope, faith in God is courage to act. Faith in God includes the courage to live, to be, even when doubt is present; it encompasses the ability to tolerate the risk and uncertainty and insecurity that are involved in living by faith and not by sight.

Just as the rival faiths to Christianity have a specific content, so does the Christian faith. Its content or ultimate concern is captured in the confessional statement that Jesus is the Christ and that he is Lord. This statement means that one has the conviction that the final power which is ultimately responsible for this universe has spoken a reconciling word to him in and through Jesus of Nazareth. The reconciling word meets me where I actually am and says that I am accepted and loved just for myself, with no strings attached. The real me, the good and bad mixture, is beloved and accepted, not the one I might become, or might have been, but the one I really am.

This word tells me that I am accepted and loved, but it says also that I am and have been afraid of this God who loves. Afraid because I have not been what I might have been and because I am aware that I will not be all that I could be. Afraid because I do not want to admit to myself what I really have made of my life, but would prefer to hide amid shameless pretensions of goodness, or would clutch to myself suitable punishment for my failure. This strange word tells me that I must give up the pretensions and the rewarding punishment; I must be who I am, a child of God, beloved just because I am a child of God. Nor does this strange word stop here; it tells me also that my life has purpose and that its purpose is discovered in loving my fellowman as an act of response to the prior love of God. It assures me that I can live because life itself is good; good because God is good, not because life has, or does, or will feel good. The future too is now no longer a cause for worry, because this God who has claimed us is the Lord of the future; tomorrow is in his hands. Whatever it brings, seeming good or ill, can be found to be meaningful and life-fulfilling because it is his gift.

Chapter V

God: Enemy or Friend

THE PREVIOUS chapters have made a case for faith as a part, indeed the central principle, of everyone's life. Further, it has been indicated how the crises of life are not merely sometime things, but part of every age and very much intensified in our age. Thus it is that no one ever lives without having the meaning of his life called into question by the very process of life itself. It is this latter experience which we call the question of God, and say, because of the crises of life and because everyone lives by faith, that this question is common to all humanity. That does not mean, however, that all raise the question in the same manner. Quite the contrary is the case; each raises the question in terms of his own unique existence because of the understanding that he already possesses and because of the nature of his personal problems.

ASKING THE GOD QUESTION

Some of the ways, however, of asking about God arise out of a context different from the one suggested here. Philosophers, for example, have always asked about God, but, as philosophers rather than individuals, they have asked it quite differently. Characteristically their question would arise not from the crises of life, but from cognition.

This cognition might lead to a definition of God such as "unmoved mover" and the question then becomes, Does such a being exist? Another philosophical manner of asking about God is to try to define or discover the nature of ultimate reality, or the first cause, or the final end. Although these are all quite legitimate intellectual questions, they are intellectual questions *about* God and as such are not *the God question*. Questions like these are not the God question because they arise dispassionately as cognitive issues and not from the depths of life itself; they are asked as questions in general and not as questions of ultimate importance to one's own self. No question is the God question unless it calls into doubt the very meaning of one's existence; such a question is always fraught with great anxiety. The God question arises when one's existing faith begins to be shaken.

At this point it is well to recall that faith is not mere intellectual assent, no simple pattern of morals, nor equal to some emotional response. Faith is, rather, something that involves the whole person; it is a centered act of the personality that expresses one's reliance upon the object of faith to make life meaningful. In this fashion, faith can be seen always to involve trust and commitment. One commits one's very life to the object of faith and trusts that life will be made meaningful because of this act, this relationship. One has a certain expectation of one's object of faith, or anticipates certain results. These attitudes of anticipation or expectation necessarily imply some understanding about the character or power of the object of faith. The communist, for example, believes that the trouble with man is the nature of his social order and that the very processes of history are moving us toward the ideal (communist) social order. Expectations such as these always accompany faith, although they may not be raised to conscious expression, and because they do, history it-self puts them to the test; the very ongoing nature of life calls these expectations into question. Arthur Koestler, in *The God That Failed,* tells us of the experience of having one's object of faith gradually shown to be incapable of living up to expectations. His story is about the failure of communism, but communism is not the only faith that is failing, as we have noted earlier.

Simply to live is to express trust and commitment, to have faith that life is worthwhile because one believes that some goal is attainable, that someone or something is worth living for. Everyone, then, devotes his life to something: that something may be happiness, power, pop-ularity, fame, family, or even the church. Whatever the object may be, our concern here is simply to note that these things can and do become the object of faith, the reason for life, the source of meaning. These faith objects may vary from time to time. In fact, few of us are ever really single-minded about our faith, but rather are mostly divided selves. But we all do have this kind of faith and relate ourselves to something upon which we depend for meaning and it is this relationship which is our actual reli-gion. " The universality of such religious faith is obscured for us. For one thing, we tend in highly institutionalized societies, such as our own, to confuse the reality of human processes with their institutional organization and expres-sion. . . . It is so with religion and religious faith and worship. We tend to confuse these with the official organ-izations and habits, with observance of special rites, with the functioning of a special leadership, and with the ex-pression of a specific faith. But religion is a much more various thing. And it is inescapable as institutions of reli-gion are not. As the faith that life is worth living, as the reference of life to a source of meaning and value, as the practice of adoration and worship, it is common to all men. For no man lives without living for some purpose, for the glorification of some god, for the advancement of some cause."[48] If we accept the understanding of faith or religion outlined above, it is clear that the question or the problem of God is universal. This, however, is no new insight, for as long ago as Martin Luther, indeed in the Biblical material itself, this understanding was present. Luther remarks: "What does it mean to have a God, or what is God? Trust and faith of the heart alone make both God and idol. . . . Whatever then thy heart clings to and relies upon, that is properly thy God."

THE DIVISIVENESS AND IDOLATRY OF THE GODS

When we recover the proper understanding of the word " god," it becomes clear that mostly we are polytheists, that is, that we have many gods. Common gods of Western civilization are nation, sex, ideology, family, society, or mankind. All these gods have a common element, their finitude. Not one of them exists in a single universal form; rather, they are culturally relative. It is perfectly clear that the worship of the nation in the United States is quite different from the worship of the nation in Russia and that these two religions are divisive, that is, they set the people of the United States against the people of Russia and vice versa. Other gods also have this divisive quality. The man who is seeking for the meaning of life in sexual expression finds himself set against those who are seeking for the meaning of life in family or in society. The one who is seeking for the meaning of life by national expression finds himself against those who are seeking for the meaning of their life by serving all of mankind. It is probably not too strong to say that every war is fought because some nation or some ideology has been elevated to the place of God and come into conflict with a rival god, for it is the gods that make life worthwhile, and when something threatens one's gods, he is ready indeed to die to preserve them. Without gods, life would not be worthwhile; this is made clear by reference again to our definition of a god as that which gives meaning to life and that on which life is centered.

Men elevate certain ideals such as equality or freedom, brotherhood or liberty, to an absolute status and regard these as the *sine qua non* of human existence. Men are then willing to die for these, but none of them are eternal values; they are exclusive instead of inclusive. Take equality as an example. Equality within the American Constitution is presumably guaranteed. When we ask for whom is it guaranteed, however, we begin to see the exclusive nature of this ideal. The proper meaning of it is equality for some only, namely, for Americans only. This equality does not extend to Europeans and especially does not extend to Orientals. If we examine the whole question more carefully, we can discover that in practice this equality is not extended even to those who are American citizens, if they happen to be of the Negro race and live in one of our Southern states. Furthermore, it is a tragic fact that the pursuit of one of these ideals may bring a person into conflict with another of these ideals. The passionate pursuit of equality may very easily jeopardize freedom. This can be seen if one looks at the history of the United States as it has pursued socioeconomic equality and has found this goal already to be in conflict with a laissez-faire understanding of freedom. The goal of equality for all has come into conflict with an earlier ideal also, i.e., the government that governs best governs least.

With the kind of observation indicated above, we can

see that modern civilization has a pantheon of gods just
as did the Greeks of old, and that our gods can and do
fight among themselves just as did the gods of the Greeks.
We fail to see that we are involved in this divisive worship, because we have lost the proper understanding of
what it is that makes a god, namely, our faith.

There is an even greater tragedy than the divisiveness
of the gods and that tragedy is that these gods are idols.
An idol is simply a substitute for the one true God. An idol
is a pretender and cannot perform its promise, because an
idol is finite. There is one great truth about this whole universe; if one observes it closely, he perceives immediately
that things come into existence, persist for a time, and
then pass out of existence. Nothing lasts, all is in flux,
everything is in process. Obviously, some things last
longer than others; the insects and the leaves live mostly
only for a season. Families live much longer, and races
longer still. But there is an end even to nations and to
civilizations. Where now is the glory of Greece, Rome, or
Egypt? One cannot protect oneself against finitude by
binding oneself to nation or race or ideology, for these
things too are doomed to destruction. The scientists say
that our solar system itself will, only in a matter of time,
pass out of existence. The idol cannot perform its promise
of giving eternal meaning, because the idol itself is a part
of temporal events. What, however, shall we call the cause
of this nature of all things, this evanescence of the world?
Shall we call it Fate or Kismet, as did men of old, thus referring to the inexplicable and mysterious end that seems
so often to overtake life in its fullness? Or shall we be
more philosophical or scientific and call this final cause
the nature of things or, simply, reality? Whatever we shall
call it, it is clear that this last power beyond the powers
abides, that things *are* the way they are.

GOD AS ENEMY

Alfred North Whitehead once said that religion was a process going from God-the-void to God-the-enemy to God-the-great-friend-and-companion. Christianity certainly speaks of God both as enemy and as friend, but how is it that Christianity can speak of God as our enemy? Francis Thompson, in his famous poem " The Hound of Heaven," tells us something of what it means to experience God as one's enemy. Thompson tells of all things in life to which he turned for meaning, only to find that there was no final meaning there, or to have them snatched away from him by the final power that rules over this life. Until at last he stands before God, crying out, " My harness piece by piece Thou hast hewn from me, and smitten me to my knee; . . . I stand amid the dust o' the mounded years "; and in a final cry of pain he objects, " Must Thy harvest-fields be dunged with rotten death?" Yet at the end of this poem stands one of the great affirmations of faith in the God who makes things the way they are, an affirmation that this God is only concerned for the ultimate welfare of man and that the darkness which one experiences in life is only the shade of his hand outstretched to give one genuine life. If one looks at life honestly, one must agree that there is much in it that appears to be one's enemy. We live in such a mysterious world; how shall one explain diseases or natural disasters? We confess the origin of these tragedies in our insurance policies when we call them " acts of God." Religiously, however, we wonder, but if we wonder honestly, we ask with William Blake, " Tiger! Tiger! burning bright In the forest of the night. . . . Did he smile his work to see? Did he who made the Lamb make thee? "

We experience human life as being bound in a limited

world not of its own making, nor of its own choosing. The limitations to human life are felt as life-negating barriers in many instances, and we cry out with Omar Khayyám, " Ah Love! could you and I with Him conspire To grasp this Sorry Scheme of Things entire, Would not we shatter it to bits—and then Remould it nearer to the Heart's Desire! " In our moments of honesty we are certain that were we God we could make a much better world than the one that has been given to us.

Man discovers that he cannot free himself of concern about the basic needs of life, those things which hold body and soul together, but neither can he make life certain and meaningful with them. Over all of life there hangs a Damocles sword and sooner or later the thread must break. Man must have fellowship and love, but perfect fellowship and love are impossible for him. In the most loving of his acts there is something of selfishness, and who is there who is ever continuously a loving person? And do we not find so often that even our best acts of love go astray and do not achieve the aim they intend? A businessman on his way home from work, as a spontaneous act of love, stops for a bouquet of roses. But how many wives can receive such a gift without wondering why it was given at this particular time?

Man has an unquenchable thirst for knowledge and for the perfection of his work, but he always ends his life with these incomplete. There is no end to what he wants to know; thus, if for no other reason, he is frustrated because of the illimitable expanse of knowledge; he is like Thomas Wolfe, who reportedly found it a traumatic experience to discover that the Harvard library was buying books more rapidly than he could read them. Man wishes to pronounce *complete* over his work, but at his end he must always recognize that there is much yet left to be done.

Man cannot escape from a sense of duty, but neither can he fulfill it; thus he is always plagued by guilt. Guilt is a universal human phenomenon, because no man ever lives up fully to his ideals; he is always short at one point or another. Furthermore, he must make choices between possibilities or ways of living his life, and the choice made *for* one means that the choice is made *against* another. This too is a source of guilt. One is always a person who could have been someone other than who he is and there is no certainty that who he is, is the correct choice.

God is he who denies every earthly security, who decrees that there shall be no hiding place from finitude. It is God who makes man for love, yet has created the world in which love is unfulfilling. God is the power who sets a boundary to all man's knowing and doing so that he must go to his tomb unfulfilled. The question to Christianity might well be then, Why speak of this enigmatic power as God? Why not call it Fate, or even the devil? May it not be that life is a cruel game? " One fate comes to all, to the righteous and the wicked, to the good and the evil, to the clean and the unclean, to him who sacrifices and him who does not. . . . One fate comes to all." (Eccl. 9:2–3.)

THE GOD OF CHRISTIANITY

No one can deny the factuality of the information suggested above. But the scandal of Christianity is that it dares to call the final power, the seeming enemy, *God our Father*. This statement of Christianity is an affirmation and a confession of faith. It affirms, first of all, that meaning is found here and here only. All human endeavor is indeed limited and thus cannot be a final source of meaning in itself. Nor can anything that is a part of this creative existence be the final source of meaning for our lives.

Christianity confesses, and professes, that despite appearances, when faith is related to this final power, we can know that he is our Father. Christianity confesses that out of a faith relationship to this final power one can receive the courage to be, the courage to live in this world. Life, all of it, can be affirmed as meaningful because of this god. It was this understanding which allowed Francis Thompson to conclude his poem " The Hound of Heaven " with his affirmation of meaning.

Christianity says that there is only One who is truly God and that everything else, when it is elevated to the status of God, is simply an idol. The God to whom Christianity points is not any part of the visible, the tangible world. The Christian God thus cannot be identified as some sort of world spirit, nor adequately worshiped simply by reverencing all of human life or even life itself. Although this God is not part of the visible and tangible world, Christianity says that he is responsibly related to the visible and tangible world. It is his world in the sense that he continually gives it life and that his relationship to it is one of loving concern. Christianity believes that God is always concerned about the world, that he is involved in its history, but also that he transcends its evanescence. Thus, there are basically two major factors to the Christian doctrine of God. First, the affirmation that the final power in control of the universe is this God, and that there is no other power to which he is subject unless he chooses to subject himself to such, and secondly, that his relationship to the world is characterized appropriately as a loving one. Doubtless there are many who would agree that there is some final power, but many would wonder why this power should be called " our Father." Why does Christianity affirm that God is trustworthy?

The first way in which one might interpret such a ques-

tion would be to construe it like this: Why put trust and
confidence in this ultimate God instead of in a lesser but
more utilitarian god, for example, some ideology or human
social system that promises us the basic needs of life? Is
not the experience of this God as the enemy of our life
enough to make us turn away to a god who will be concerned with the happiness of men? Must not man turn
away from this life, denying the God of Christianity, to
the gods of this world who will provide him with earthly
bread, earthly love, and earthly worship? What is wrong
with being a materialist, that is, believing that man is a
socioeconomic animal? In answer to questions like these,
Christianity must again point to the fact that the gods of
this world are not ultimate; that they do not transcend
finite existence. Each of them is limited, competitive, and
thus divides mankind into warring camps. Man may even
become a divided creature within himself and destroy
himself psychologically. Each of these earthly gods is
doomed to annihilation, and thus any fulfillment that it
promises is ultimately false. For these reasons, says Christianity, the ultimate God is the only power that transcends
divisive finitude. Only if the power beyond the powers
can be trusted is it possible for one to say that there is
ultimate meaning to human life. The question of God in
this sense then becomes, Is he trustworthy?

We must now try to understand why it is that man
questions the trustworthiness of God. To find out why
man has doubt we must first of all find out what it means
to doubt God. In the light of the understanding of faith
that has been developed earlier, doubt means actually
putting one's trust in something other than God. Doubting
the trustworthiness of God or doubting God is part and
parcel of trusting in some other god. In the process of life
one must always choose his god or gods. Life is always

putting before us situations that demand decision, and in the quality of decision we reflect the loyalty to the god we have chosen. There is no possibility of bringing life to a halt so that we do not have to make these decisions, so that our choice can be held in abeyance while we have time to think out more clearly which god we will choose. The very ongoing nature of life forces us to make our choice time and time again.

In a more profound sense, questioning the trustworthiness of God means to begin to wonder if life itself is really worthwhile. As a person grows older and sees a wrinkle-lined face and gray-streaked hair staring back at him from the mirror, it is easy for a subtle doubt to creep in, doubtfulness that the goals which were so bright and shining when life was new are ever achievable or even worthwhile. Thus, the woman who sees her children grown and her beauty gone may wonder what life has left for her. The man who suddenly wakes up to find himself sixty-five and retired, whether or not he wishes to be, may wonder if there are anything but declining years left for him. The thought arises that if all is vanity, as Ecclesiastes says, why bother to go on living? Why not just give up and die?

The kind of doubt described above we shall term existential doubt, and we should recognize that it rests in many of our ways of thinking about our lives. It can creep upon us as simply as the daily thought that basically the world works against life for us. When one is filled with the joy of a task just completed and well done, this doubt may be temporarily overcome, but soon there is another task to be done, or the one recently completed is to be done over again, and then the doubt begins. Why should the world be such that we have to do things over and over again? Why must one be sentenced to a lifetime of cleaning the house only to have it get dirty almost immediately? Why must things always be wearing out and having to be replaced? Has not God set for us in life a task as tortuous as that one given to Sisyphus of old? And is there really any such thing as human freedom and responsibility? Perhaps life is just a joke and we are all nothing more than complex machines. Could not the scientific determinists be right when they say that there is no such thing as human freedom? Thoughts like these, whether expressed or unexpressed, lurk in many of our ways of thinking or feeling about our daily lives and in each case represent an existential doubt of God.

But why really does man begin to doubt God? Why can he not continue in a pattern of trustfulness? It was suggested above, from the understanding of faith developed earlier, that in the first instance, doubting God simply meant actually putting one's trust in something else. When one trusts something less than God, however, it means that one must surely be brought to earth sooner or later, because anything less than God is a part of the creation and thus is finite. When he trusts in anything less than God, man must inevitably be disappointed. When one's idol collapses, he falls into deep despair; he is stricken with grief; life itself seems to hold little if any meaning for him. This state of grief or despair lasts until one can grasp hold of some other god that will promise to make life meaningful again. And thus it is, with the idolatrous process of life, man goes from one idol to another as these are snatched away from him, and as each is taken from him he experiences despair, anxiety, meaninglessness. When his idols fail him, at that precise moment, man cries out that life itself is no good, and thus, that the true giver of life could not possibly love him. Man doubts God's trustworthiness because his idols fail him. At the point of the failure of his idols it is possible for man to trust in God, but not until he gives up his idols. Is trust in God then impossible?

Man distrusts life and the God who gives it because man's idols fail, but how is it that man can come to trust in God? First of all, man must come to understand himself as an idolater. He must become aware and admit precisely who he is. Presumably this is what earlier evangelistic religion had in mind when it spoke of "a sense of sin." The mourners' bench at the front of the church building was there for those who had come to know that their real problem was their own idolatrous relationship to the gods of this world. Until one is aware that he really has given himself into the hands of his idols, there is no escape. An analogous situation is suggested by the requirement of Alcoholics Anonymous that a man must admit that alcohol has defeated him before he can be helped. Our unknown idolatry keeps us imprisoned. Idols will always enslave us until we become aware of our enslavement.

Both the Old Testament and the New Testament point out the nature of man's problem with considerable clarity. In Genesis the story of Adam and Eve, the Garden, the serpent, and the two trees is the story of the birth of our idolatry. When Adam awakened to life it was to life in the right relationship with God. It was genuine life represented by free access to the tree of life. Adam and Eve are not alienated from each other, nor are they alienated from life itself, because they are not alienated from God. But the scene includes another possibility shown to us in the presence of the tree of the knowledge of good and evil, to which there is free access, but from which they are forbidden to eat lest they die. Free access to the fruit of the knowledge of good and evil suggests that there always hangs over man's head the terrifying possibility of refusing to accept his life itself as a good gift. At any moment man may cease to accept himself, his own existence, as having its value built in by virtue of the giver of all gifts, and he may begin to look for some means to justify his existence, some way to assure himself that life is worthwhile. The presence of the serpent in the story and the suggestions that the serpent makes indicate that the doubt of God and the doubt of the meaningfulness of life go together. To eat of the fruit of the knowledge of good and evil means to take in one's own hands the decision as to what it is that makes life ultimately meaningful or meaningless and this is nothing more nor less than the choice of a god. When the fruit is eaten, life itself is divided into categories of good and evil. Life is no longer automatically acceptable; one has to look for some reason to make it acceptable; one has to be assured that life is good. Once one begins to doubt the meaningfulness of life, however, one no longer has free access to the tree of life. The quality of oneness with self, with fellowman, is shattered because the quality of oneness with God is shattered.

The story in Genesis is not just a story of two people long long ago, but is a story of you and me, of every man. The New Testament reaffirms this story as the story of every man's life, as Paul writes in Rom. 1:19–23: "For what can be known about God is plain to them, because God has shown it to them. Ever since the creation of the world his invisible nature, namely, his eternal power and deity, has been clearly perceived in the things that have been made. So they are without excuse; for although they knew God they did not honor him as God or give thanks to him, but they became futile in their thinking, and their senseless minds were darkened. Claiming to be wise, they became fools, and exchanged the glory of the immortal

God for images resembling mortal man or birds or animals or reptiles." These Biblical accounts, then, refer to perennial experiences of mankind. Man is always and forever waking up to find himself outside the garden, incomplete, driven to know that his work does not produce salvation. The point of all this is that life itself has built in it the ability to convict us of our idolatry. No man lives without this sense of incompleteness because no man is complete apart from God. Being convicted of idolatry is a complex process that must include all the aspects of man's personality. Furthermore, there must be included within this process an assurance that the one who strips one's idols away is the loving God in whom the true meaning of life can be found.

How does this happen? H. Richard Niebuhr writes: " It does not happen without the struggle of his reason. For by reason he discovers the inadequacy of all his gods and is driven to despair in life's meaning. It does not happen without experience, without the experience of frustration, of noting the death of all things, the experience of the internal division in which his various worship involves him, the experience of the great social catastrophes which show the weakness of the great causes and beings in which he trusted as saviors of life. It does not happen without the operation of something we must call spiritual, something which is like the intuition of the thinker, like the creative insight of the artist, like the flash of recognition of truth. All these elements are involved. Furthermore, this transfer of faith to the ultimate being does not take place without moral struggle, without recognition of the unworthiness both of our transgressions and our obediences to our moral laws."[49]

This last sentence of Niebuhr's is an important clue, for the conviction of idolatry must extend to the greatest of man's efforts, namely, to his religion and to his personal goodness, for these creations are a basic part of man's efforts to justify himself, to assure himself that life is meaningful on the basis of certain works to which he can point. Karl Barth also has reminded us very wisely and very extensively that man's most successful escape from God is in religion. Until one despairs finally and completely of his own religious effort, of his own moral efforts, he cannot understand truly that he falls under the judgment expressed by the apostle Paul, " None is righteous, no not one." Until one truly despairs of his own goodness, he cannot possibly understand the words of Jesus, " Why do you call me good? No one is good but God alone " (Mark 10:18).

God alone is good, but the goodness of God is a mysterious good. His goodness is beyond our understanding, because our understanding itself is corrupted by our desire to judge what is good and what is evil. As Karl Barth reminds us, " there is no good and evil ' in itself,' but God judges good and evil."[50] Thus we cannot understand the God who sends his rain on the just and the unjust alike. If we were doing it, would we not send the appropriate amount of rain and a disproportionate amount, either more or less, to those who were evil? Does the evil farmer really deserve the same treatment as the good farmer? Our answer must be that we do not feel that he deserves it. The mystery of God's goodness is further developed in one of Jesus' parables about a man who hires workers for his farm early in the morning and late in the afternoon. The strangeness of this man is that he pays equal wages to those who are hired early in the morning and those who worked only one hour in the late afternoon; each receives the same total reward. Again we find ourselves resentful of this kind of indiscriminate goodness, because our good-

ness is not like that. Furthermore, the judgment of God
cannot be seen in the misfortunes of this world; in fact,
the very word " misfortune " is a creation of our grasping
at the categories of good and evil. It was common with
the Jews of Jesus' time to think that misfortune represented punishment for sin, but Jesus insisted that there
was only one class of men, all stood under the category of
sin and must repent in order to receive salvation. As Jesus
put it in Luke 13:4–5: " Or those eighteen upon whom
the tower in Siloam fell and killed them, do you think
that they were worse offenders than all the others who
dwelt in Jerusalem? I tell you, No; but unless you repent
you will all likewise perish."

Before man can repent of his sin he must recognize that
his final assault on infinity, his ultimate attempt to outwit
finitude by building a tower to heaven, namely, his own
goodness, character development, social perfection, all
human effort, in fact, ends incomplete. Only when man is
ready radically to abandon his own efforts at salvation is
he ready for trust in God. As the psalmist put it: " In my
distress I called upon the Lord. . . . From his temple he
heard my voice, and my cry to him reached his ears. . . .
He delivered me " (Ps. 18:6, 17). In ultimate despair that
his own works can make life meaningful, it becomes possible for man to respond to the ever-present invitation of
God to faith.

At the point of his own failure, man can understand that
salvation is not a matter of his own success. When he is
willing to abandon self-dependence, because he recog-
nizes it as undependable, then man can also hear God's
word inviting him to dependence upon God and trust in
him alone. Upon this invitation and by virtue of this invitation man can trust in God. Because this trust is not
based upon human reason, logic, or knowledge we must

call it a leap of faith. This leap of faith reverses the relationship of man to the two trees in the garden, not that
man has arrived at the goal of faith, but that he has begun. This is the first rejection of the knowledge of good
and evil, and with the rejection he experiences LIFE. He
understands that it was and is his sin, his judging of good
and evil, which creates the categories of good things and
evil things. But now, believing in the fatherly love of God,
he can be thankful for all things in life, for all things are
given by God. As the Heidelberg Catechism puts it, Part
27, " All things come not by chance, but by his fatherly
hand." Good and evil then can no longer be considered in
and of themselves as ways of evaluating the worthwhileness of life. The worthwhileness of life is determined by
the fatherly goodness of God. But can we truly affirm life
as ALL GOOD? " Now what shall we say of wicked men
and devils? Shall we say that they too are subject to God?
Although he does not govern them by his Spirit, yet he
checks them by his power, as with a bridle, so that they
are unable even to move unless he permits them to do so.
Further, he even makes them ministers of his will, so that
they are forced, unwilling and against their inclination, to
effect what seems good to him.

" What benefit accrues to you from the knowledge of
this? Very much. For it would go ill with us, if anything
were permitted wicked men and devils without the will
of God; then our minds could never be tranquil, for thinking ourselves exposed to their pleasure. Only then do we
safely rest when we know them to be curbed by the will
of God and, as it were, held in confinement, so that they
cannot do anything but by his permission, especially since
God himself undertakes to be our guardian and the cap-
tain of our salvation."[51]

A radical trust in God means a radical distrust in *my*

knowledge of good and evil, insofar as these have to do with the meaningfulness of life. My feelings and thoughts as to what would make my life worthwhile are not trustworthy! Finding meaning in life is not based upon achieving a certain kind of success, nor arriving at a certain emotional state. Meaningfulness arises out of trusting in the God who makes himself known as the only God who transcends the finitude of this world. In a sense we must say that life comes out of the death of all purely human hopes. It is out of the death of my trust in myself, my trust in human creations or ideologies, that life can come. One must experience the death of all things before he can understand that all things are alive. Or, to put it conversely, one comes to understand that living by trust in self or idols is what is really meant by DEATH. The death that God spoke about to Adam and Eve as the inevitable result of eating from the tree of the fruit of the knowledge of good and evil was not physical death, but the death of alienation from God, the death of meaninglessness. It is this death of meaninglessness of which the early Christians spoke when they said, " We were dead, but now we are alive," or again, " We have passed out of death into life." Through the ministry of Jesus Christ they had become aware of what death really was: alienation from God.

When we understand that mankind is continually seeking to save himself, to secure his own existence by his own means, but that because of his finitude he must always fail in this task, then we can understand the meaning of John 12:25: " He who loves his life loses it, and he who hates his life in this world will keep it for eternal life." This passage does not mean that one must continue to detest his existence in order to be saved, but that he must rather give up his idols as ways of salvation. The *giving up* of idols, the *giving up* of seeking to preserve life by holding on to it and grasping after it is always folly to those who are still eating the fruit of the knowledge of good and evil. Hidden idolatry always blinds us to the truth and prevents our acceptance of life. " Whoever seeks to gain his life will lose it, but whoever loses his life will preserve it." (Luke 17:33.)

Chapter VI

Jesus Christ, History and Symbol

IN THIS CHAPTER and the next, attention will be given to three closely interrelated items: the way in which Christian faith becomes possible for an individual, the Christ event, and Biblical interpretation. At this point a brief summary of the meaning of Christian faith developed in the earlier chapters seems necessary.

CHRISTIAN SELF-UNDERSTANDING

Faith, viewed simply as a human phenomenon, is that which serves as the ordering center of human personality; it is that which accounts for a person's being who he is and as he is. As such, faith cannot be equated with any one facet or function of human personality; it transcends and unifies emotion, will, and intellect to make man a functioning whole. Faith is held, whether consciously or unconsciously, in some kind of symbolic pattern. Faith may be expressed as an ultimate trust and loyalty in its object. There may be an infinite variety of objects of faith, and Christian faith is distinguished as that faith which places ultimate trust and loyalty in the final power that is responsible for the whole creation, but not identical with it.

Paul Tillich refers to this final power as " being itself " or " the ground of being " or as the " God above the God of theism " or finally as " the God who appears when God has disappeared in the anxiety of doubt."[52] H. Richard Niebuhr refers to this final power as " this reality, this way things are," or " the source of all things and the end of all " or the " God beyond the gods," and remarks that the strange thing about the history of Christians is that they have been enabled to call this particular reality their God.[53] Rudolf Bultmann speaks of this final power as that which " makes man finite, who makes a comedy of man's care, who allows his longing to miscarry, who casts him into solitude, who sets a terminus to all his knowing and doing, who calls him to duty and who gives the guilty over to torment. . . . It is God who forces man into life and drives him into care, . . . the enigmatic power beyond time, yet master of the temporal; beyond being, yet working in it."[54] It is this power which Christianity means when it says God! Much more can and must be said, but unless it is clear that Christianity affirms as God this final, responsible, and insurmountable power, then anything else that is said is meaningless.

Christian faith at its base, then, is an affirmation of confidence, trust, and loyalty in this final power. Such a faith is expressed as a profound trust in life itself, for life is God's gift to each one, moment by moment. This profound trust in life does not appear to be natural to man. Rather, one can come to this point only when one has experienced the failure of one's other gods, one's idols. So long as one's idols function, one will not believe them ultimately impotent and untrustworthy. Supreme among the idols created by man is religion, the religion by which man seeks to justify himself and to reassure himself. All contemporary theologians are in agreement at this point as perhaps at no other, but most of all Karl Barth has led the way in denouncing this last stronghold of man, for it is a strong-

hold *against* God. More than thirty-five years ago Barth
declared that " the polemic of the Bible, unlike that of the
religions, is directed not against the godless world, but
against the *religious* world, whether it worships under the
auspices of Baal or of Jehovah. . . ."[55] Religion is the high-
est attainment of man, but it is a snare and a delusion, for
in it " sin celebrates its triumph."[56] " So deeply does it
[sin] penetrate every human capacity that the attempt to
elude it by taking up with religion entangles us more
surely in its guilt and plunges us into the destiny of
death."[57] Religion is a snare and a delusion because it lets
man think that he is seeking for God, that he has some attainment in righteousness of his own, that his act of worship is a service to God and a guarantee of security. Until
all this is seen to be sham and pretense, not the worship of
God but the worship of the creature, man will continue in
his delusion, ensnared in false worship.

Religion aids and abets man in making demands upon
life that it not be what it is, but that it be what he wishes
it were. In the guise of the promise of heaven, religion
allows man to condemn and despise the actual life that
God has given him. By practicing religion in the form of
church attendance, committee work, and generous giving,
one can easily condemn the God who claims him through
a beastly neighbor, an employee crying out for reasonable
treatment, or a forgotten minority restively waiting for
long delayed justice. Nels Ferré, in a provocative work
written a decade ago, suggested that man's relation to
God could be well described in a metaphor of the sun and
the umbrella. Man raises various umbrellas to shelter himself from the sun, and then lives in darkness, for the sun
is his only light. Ferré suggested that religious man makes
the church, Christ, and the Bible into shelters from God.
Ferré's metaphor is correct up to a point; its failure is that

there can be no real escape from the God who is God. One always lives in relation to God, for God is the very ground of existence, but one may live in rebellion or in trust, and he may cloak his rebellion with wrappings that make it seem to be a genuine relationship of trust. The religious efforts of man are precisely this; they are attempts to cloak man's efforts to establish his own security with a garb of piety so that they will seem to lie within the security that faith in God alone can give.

Trusting in this God who is God means giving up our right to pronounce good and evil over our own existence. We make this pronouncement of good and evil from our deepest faith, and its outpouring is a conviction about the reason and worthwhileness of our lives. Faith in God is no more a saccharine profession that all is sweetness and light than it is a raging denouncement of the tyrant who gives life the way it is. The man who denies or explains away the existence of suffering and evil as only appearances is sadly deluded. Many so-called Christians fall into this trap and live a life of lies, pretending to experience life or feel about it in a way that neither they nor anyone else actually experiences or feels.

The first step toward reconciliation with God is a ruthless self-honesty. But a full trust in God means giving up the right to pronounce any final good or evil over one's own life—or anyone else's, for that matter. Life is neither good nor evil because of any earthly circumstances. Ultimately, there are no such categories as good fortune or ill fortune; fortune is a pagan goddess who must be put aside. It is not within our capacity, not within our knowledge, to say "life is unfulfilled if . . ." and add our own prescription for a meaningless existence. Certainly one may *feel* meaninglessness, may feel there is no sense of purpose or ultimate quality to human life, but this is like the child who needs to cry without knowing why. Our feeling is not an adequate basis for evaluating the universe; nonetheless, it is our feeling and it must not be hidden under pious lies. Paul Tillich has made the point very well that the anxiety of meaninglessness can be borne, not by trying to pretend that it is not true, but by becoming aware of the God beyond the God of theism. It is this God who is proclaimed by the " Crucified who cried to God who remained his God after the God of confidence had left him in the darkness of doubt and meaninglessness."[58] Seemingly, it is only at the last frontier of every human possibility, where every human possibility is shown to be insufficient, where death and meaninglessness reign supreme, where the God of theism and confidence vanishes before the abyss of nothingness; it is only here that the God who is God makes himself known. It is only here because only at this point is man willing, or daring enough, or desperate enough, really to face the God question, Does human existence have any real meaning at all? Until the question is asked out of the desperation of one who faces nothingness, the God who is God cannot make himself known.

The new life of which the New Testament so confidently speaks comes only out of death, not death in the usual sense, but the death of human self-striving and eternal hopes in human remedies, the death of man's struggle for self-justification and visible salvation. Contact with the God who is God means judgment, enlightenment, and redemption. No one likes to come to this place, for it means the end of dreams; it means disillusionment; it means accepting the unacceptable, oneself and one's world. " For this reason, the Gospel of Christ is a shattering disturbance, an assault which brings everything into question."[59] The enlightenment is revelation, an opening onto oneself and one's actual relation to God the very ground of being. This revelation offers a new possibility, a new self-understanding, a new relationship to God. One can now see that what he has always called life is really death, and what he has called death is really life. He has been one of those blind ones who thought he could see; he has espoused the world and called it God. Now the only possibility is shown to be dying to the world that one may live to God. The new self-understanding is precisely that he who seeks to save his life will lose it.

BIBLICAL SYMBOLS

The question to which we now turn is how this new understanding comes about and what it has to do with Jesus Christ. Our problem is to see the relationship of the Biblical symbols to the new self-understanding.

There was a time when it was assumed quite uncritically that the Bible reported literal history in some objective fashion. It was further generally believed that faith was based on these events *as* historical, photographable, tape-recordable events. Miracles were held in high esteem as proof of the deity of Jesus, and the words in the New Testament attributed to him were assumed to be quite literally his words, recorded as spoken. Most of the traditional theology of the church and most of its popular theology today is based on principles of Biblical interpretation that make these assumptions. Needless to say, such assumptions do not vitiate all the theological statements, but they do call for a radical rethinking in the light of the present state of Biblical studies.

The revolution in Biblical studies began some two centuries ago with a Frenchman, Jean Astruc, who discovered the two basic strands of thought and/or authorship in

Genesis. Thus even in the eighteenth century, literalism was threatened as a valid method of Biblical interpretation, but as late as 1925, America was rocked by the battle between William Jennings Bryan, a literalist, and Clarence Darrow in the Scopes "Monkey Trial." Bryan made such ridiculous statements as asserting that he believed the whale swallowed Jonah, and if the Bible said it, he would believe Jonah had swallowed the whale. Since 1925, America has largely abandoned literalism, but has by no means begun to catch up with the whole field of Biblical scholarship, which has had two revolutionary developments since that time. The first was the theory of form criticism, the second, demythologization.

As critical study of the Bible progressed during the nineteenth century, it became clear that the Bible could not be read like the morning newspaper. Gradually the history of the ancient period was unrolled and the method of development of Biblical books began to emerge. It became evident that the Bible contained some history, some legend, and some myth. In the mid-1920's, mainly through the work of Rudolf Bultmann, the theory was advanced that previous to the writing of the Gospels, during the period of oral tradition, the stories contained in the Gospels developed through certain changes. These changes could be studied by means of comparison with other oral tradition, and theories developed as to what changes would be made. Changes were due to the theological convictions and needs of the community using the stories and varied with the form that the stories took. Several basic forms were detected and given names, and ideas were developed as to the nature of the communities using these stories. From these theories about the changes in stories it was then hoped that one could progress backward from the present stories in the Gospels nearer to the actual testimony of the eyewitnesses and to the original words of Jesus.

As the world of Biblical scholarship concentrated on the thesis and task enunciated by Bultmann, it became increasingly apparent that the Gospels indeed did not represent an original unbiased account. They were composed by men whose task was dominated by their theological convictions, which in turn were affected by the theological community of which they were a part. Some scholars became radically skeptical that any part of the Gospels could be known to be a valid historical account and even the more conservative agreed that historical certainty was now only a matter of high probability. Old Testament scholars too were involved in the task of form criticism, for it was clear that the documents of the Old Testament had likewise undergone a period of oral tradition before being more securely fixed in written form.

Much earlier, certain liberal scholars had recognized what they believed to be mythological elements in the Biblical writings, and their attempt to deal with these had consisted in the elimination of suspected mythical elements. In due course their answer was shown to be untenable, but their problem became all the more urgent when the results of form criticism, instead of giving access to the actual life and words of Jesus, made it clear that the Gospels had a kerygmatic character, i.e., were books in which faith shaped fact. Foremost in facing this problem squarely and attempting to meet it was Rudolf Bultmann. His original manifesto, *New Testament and Mythology,* published during the Second World War, has become the genesis of the central problem of New Testament theology today.[60]

Bultmann contends that the New Testament was written by people who understood their whole world differently from the way modern man does; the Biblical way of understanding he calls mythological. The essence of mythological thinking, as Bultmann sees it, is that it objectifies and personifies unseen and impersonal (or transpersonal) powers. For example, a man who is out of his mind is believed to be possessed by demons. The evils of society may be accounted for by mysterious semidivine principalities and powers who are given control of the world. Messages from God are brought by physical beings called angels, which is the Greek word for " messenger." Man is viewed as ruled by these external powers; he is not autonomous. In general, acts of God are given a this-worldly description as if they were alongside other events of this world. Our problem today is, then, to discover what these stories of the Bible are saying *so that we can express it in other words*. It is rather like a problem in translation or in cryptography.

The net result of these developments in Biblical studies is that we have to see the Bible as an entirely different kind of book from that which our forefathers saw. We cannot read it as literal history at all, or perhaps we should say only where it intends so to be read, and that this is seldom. Throughout, however, it can now be seen that the Bible writers were wrestling with the ultimate questions of life. They were asking and talking about the meaning and purposes of life, what makes it worthwhile and what can be trusted. We must ask these kinds of questions of the Bible then, and not go to it for scientific kinds of information, which, for the most part, it is not capable of providing.

In an earlier chapter it was suggested that we understand ourselves in terms of symbols. Our faith, when it is thought or expressed, is thought or expressed in symbolic terms. It can be said, then, that we live by or before symbols which we believe express our deepest convictions about life. Belief as used in this sentence, however, need not mean conscious or self-conscious belief, for, as has been indicated, faith may proceed at a level of unawareness. Nonetheless, symbols do sum up our understanding of life, our faith and, further, as a means of communication have a very basic role in creating faith.

The point to be made here, however, is that the Bible too expresses itself in symbols. These Biblical symbols, like all symbolic structures, may be a word or a complex of words, which sum up a whole understanding of life. The Genesis story of Adam and Eve is a complex of words, a story, which captures an understanding of the human situation and explains it in terms of its relation to God the giver of life. The cross or the crucifix are likewise symbols, but are single-word symbols, which sum up an understanding of life.

In another dimension, the Biblical symbols, like any symbols, may be material or abstract or both, and over a period of time may change from material to abstract. A flag, although it is a material object, is an abstract symbol. Father and mother are material symbols, but as idealized may become more abstract. Sexual symbols, although originating as fully material symbols, are soon elaborated into abstract symbols by the play of fantasy. There is a sense in which every symbol has its roots in actual human history, so that it can never be considered fully abstract, except of course for purely logical symbols, created with the express purpose of meaning only what we say they mean, such as algebraic symbols. In the Bible, the exodus began as a historical event and as such may be called a material symbol, and it soon became part of the means of self-understanding of the people of Israel. The process of abstraction began with the elaboration of this actual event into an account of how Israel was known to be God's chosen people. Presumably such stories as the Adam and Eve cycle, or the prodigal son parable were abstractions from the outset, although painted with colors drawn from actual human experience. Their function from the beginning was to call to mind, or to set before man, a way of thinking about himself before God and of thinking about God; the second no less than the first.

The truth or falsity of symbolic structures must be evaluated in terms of their purpose. The purpose of the Biblical symbols is to answer real questions about life's ultimate purpose or meaning and not primarily or particularly to record the historical sequence of events, except as this in itself serves to reveal the meaning of life. The Biblical stories, then, are concerned with questions of faith rather than fact. Their truth is to be assessed, not on the basis of how well they agree with archaeology or other scientific findings, but only as to whether they tell the truth about life. This latter question is one of much more importance and of incredible difficulty. We are not in a position to say, on some basis or other, that something tells us the truth about life or that it doesn't; we can only affirm our own faith by saying that it does or doesn't for us. One simply does not decide the validity of ultimates by appealing to other ultimates. What a person affirms as the meaning of his own existence is his faith; it is his ultimate, and to affirm it on the basis of some other ultimate is really to confess that not the first, but the second, is one's ultimate.

For the Christian, one simple way to confess the meaning of his existence is to say, " Jesus Christ is Lord." These words have then become a symbol by which he expresses a certain understanding, a certain faith, as to the ultimate meaning of life. Behind the words, of course, there stands the whole history of the Christian church, but more yet, the whole life of Jesus of Nazareth. Our concern is to discover how Jesus Christ came to be associated with the new self-understanding which has been summarized in this chapter.

THE OLD TESTAMENT BACKGROUND

The name Christ is, of course, a title given to Jesus, which has its roots in the Old Testament. Christ is the Greek form of the Hebrew word transliterated *Messiah* and it means the "*Anointed One.*" It is beyond the scope of this book to consider in any detail the development of the messianic idea in Judaism; all we can do is trace the barest outlines.[61] The original meaning of the word has to do with a ceremony in which one is anointed with oil to set him apart to some office. In later Judaism the word already stood for an idea with eschatological overtones; it referred to one who was to come who would inaugurate the last times, bringing judgment and salvation. In the early stages of Israel's history an anointed one was primarily a priest-king. As a priest-king he represented the people before God, led in worship, spoke to God on behalf of the people, and ruled God's people on his behalf. Mowinckel states that "the eschatological Messiah derived his name from the sacral title of the ancient kings of Israel."[62]

In ancient Israel the task of the king was understood as that of one who rules God's people on his behalf, delivers them from their enemies, ministers justice among them, and bestows good fortune upon them by his leadership.[63] Insofar as the king is God's chosen and anointed, he is more than just an ordinary man; he is endowed with God's spirit and is in some sense thereby a divine being.

On the other hand, the king also sums up in his own being the whole of the people in their relationship to God. " Both as representative of the people, and in virtue of Yahweh's choice of him, of his sonship, his divine equipment, and his sacred character, the king of Israel-Judah (like kings everywhere else in the ancient East) was clearly the mediator between his God and his people."[64] As mediator, the king is the channel of communication between God and the people and the bearer of God's word, judgment, and salvation. A moral emphasis is to be observed also. If the king is righteous, he is blessed and the whole people with him, but if he is not righteous, following after false gods, then the whole people are led astray and fall into evil and misfortune. From this it can be seen that the king's relation to God is not conceived as a metaphysical one, but a relationship of faith and adoption. " You are my son, today I have begotten you " are the words Yahweh speaks to his chosen king.[65] Psalm 72, which is a prayer of intercession and a confession of faith, is a summary of what is desired and expected of a righteous king.

This ideal for the king of Israel from its outset incorporated certain future hopes, for no king, obviously, could embody all the virtues and blessings noted above. Further, it seems logical, as Mowinckel thinks, that through its connection with the cultus, the kingly ideal " crystallized into a present expectation and a specific promise of a definite person, who had already come or would come soon, and who was supposed to be the full realization of the ideal."[66] As part of the kingly ideal, however, it is probably incorrect to apply to these ideas of a future king the name of messianic hopes. These ideas must be seen, rather, as the backdrop and ground out of which the hopes for a Messiah arose.

It is not possible to discuss the difficult issue as to whether or not the first messianic hopes were eschatological in nature, but rather this discussion must be restricted to a discussion of the development of messianic hopes, which did in fact at some time become eschatological. The more specific occasion for the growth of the hope of a Messiah seems to have been the destruction of Israel and the captivity in Babylon. The hope at that point began to take on the character of a restoration, a deliverance, and thus logically would bring to mind the condition when God first made himself known to Israel as deliverer, the exodus. The ideas and hopes that had clustered around the person of the king were transferred into the future and to them was added the characteristic of deliverance or restoration. Reflection on God as deliverer in the exodus event brings to mind also the role of Moses. Klausner thinks that the fundamental spiritual-ethical characteristics of messianic expectation probably derive from the connection with Moses, who exemplified such characteristics,[67] but more important is the usage of David as a prototype for the future Messiah. When the question was asked, " What will Messiah be like? " the answer was found in terms of a king like David, for David was even greater in memory than actuality, and it was under his kingship that Israel remembered the most brilliant hour in her history.[68]

We may summarize nicely the Old Testament picture of the Messiah by quoting John Priest:

" Messianic thought largely grows out of the figure of the king, and the king needs to be understood in terms of his role in the cult, a role which is illustrated and amplified by a study of non-Israelite culture. This mytho-cultic origin notwithstanding, Hebrew messianism historically was attached to an ideal past king, David, and the picture of the future king was normatively shaped by this historical lineage. Historical vicissitudes and development of thought, influenced in part by foreign ideas, transmuted the historical ' messianism ' into hope for an eschatological Messianic king. Even this 'future king,' however, was dominantly influenced by the past Hebrew ideal of kingship and all that that ideal embodied. Along with this Davidic Messianism however, there emerged other ideas, which, while perhaps not originally technically Messianic in character, nevertheless played an increasingly important role in Jewish eschatological (and ultimately) messianic hopes."[69]

At this point we must note one other element in the Old Testament which at some date was associated with the Messiah, the Suffering Servant motif. Some scholars believe that the servant is only slightly connected with the kingly figure; however, even these scholars think that there is some connection. "Admittedly, the Servant has this formal connexion with the future king or ' Messiah,' that he is associated with the realization of the future hope. But in this he plays a part which far exceeds what is usually ascribed to the future king, in that he is not merely a leading figure in the restored nation, but is himself directly instrumental in the restoration of Israel, and cooperates in the fulfillment of the future hope."[70] Further, as Mowinckel notes, " It is by his proclamation of the true religion that the servant becomes a light of the nations, and the means of establishing right conditions in Israel and to the ends of the earth."[71] Bentzen is much stronger in his identification of the servant with the king; and in particular stresses the importance of the suffering aspect of the servant as depicted in Isaiah and Jeremiah.

"What is most remarkable, however, is the personal form of the ' Messianic ' preaching in these chapters. The

Prophet has not only visualized the programme of vicarious suffering; he has seen it as a personal obligation. It has become his ' Call,' just as centuries later it became the ' Call ' of Jesus.

" The prophet, like Jesus, emphasized the aspect of suffering. This ' aspect ' belongs also, as is continually and rightly stressed by Engnell, to the ancient king mythology; in our view, this is because it belongs to the myth of ' First Man,' which was the earlier prefiguration outside Israel of the description of the Sufferers in the Psalms and in Isaiah 49, 50, and 53. This is to be combined as well with Deutero-Isaiah's personal life. As the problem of unmerited suffering became *the* problem in the life of Jeremiah, so, too, it was the problem in the life of the Prophet of the Return. He saw its solution in the idea of vicarious suffering. Such was God's will (53:10). The king of Israel became the Servant of all, making intercession for them as guilt offering and in prayer, in the future of the new prophetic Moses."[72]

As we have indicated above, the hope of Israel became increasingly futuristic and at some point can be called eschatological. The precise manner or date of such a change is beyond the scope of this discussion; it is enough to note here its connection with the dualism of this age and the age to come which developed in later Judaism. It is probable that Bultmann is correct in his view that this pessimistic dualism developed under the impact of the disasters of the captivity and of the influence of Babylonian and Persian mythology. " This earth, the scene of so much distress and misery, sickness and death, sin and violence, is the habitat of evil spirits with Satan at their head, opposing the sovereignty of God. The power of darkness makes war on the power of light."[73] The history of the world is thus divided into this age and an age to come, and in the apocalyptic writers the idea is expressed that the turning point between the ages is near at hand. When the end approaches, there will be certain signs and its arrival will be a time of judgment as well as salvation. Fantasy was allowed free reign in elaborating the details of this end day, but the central items were judgment and redemption.[74] The righteous enter into the joys prepared for them, and the unrighteous face destruction or torment. " In the new age proper there is no place for the Messiah as the national king. Instead of him, there emerges a new figure, the supernatural agent of redemption who is to appear at the end of the days to inaugurate the new age. This figure bears the enigmatic title ' Man.' "[75] At a still later date this new figure combines the functions of judge and redeemer. It is with this background that we turn to the actual life of Jesus to examine how he came to be called the Christ.

How Jesus Came to Be Called the Christ

The emphases that must be remembered from the above material are those of judgment and redemption as occurring actually at the hand of an agent who is historically present, for it was this kind of experience which some who companied with Jesus claimed to have had at his hand. Most of those who knew Jesus did not see the Messiah in him. The Jews as a whole rejected him and any claims made for him or by him to be Messiah. They did so, likely because they could not see that he had or intended to transform the earthly order in the slightest. The traditional Judaistic expectation was for a national, political, this-worldly Messiah, and Jesus in no sense fitted that expectation. It is further possible to claim that Jesus directed his ministry consciously to include the Gentiles and that he left this instruction with his disciples.[76] Such an emphasis in the ministry of Jesus scandalized the

Jewish leaders, represented a judgment upon their religious exclusivism, which restricted the Kingdom of God to Jews and converts. It is perhaps not too strong to suggest that this religious conflict was a root cause of the Jewish leaders' plot to do away with Jesus. In any case, such a plot was made and carried out in a fashion which indicates that they wished to make it clear to the world that he was no Messiah. Nonetheless, after his death, a stubborn faith remained and grew among some of his followers that he was in fact Messiah, the Christ.

It seems clear that such a claim was not based upon speculation alone, whether or not it was grounded in Old Testament thought. A claim of this nature which survives the most radical disposition of its leader must be grounded in actual experience on the part of those who make it. The followers of Jesus proclaimed him Christ because he had fulfilled that function for them. The definition of Messiah or Christ being used here is a functional one; to be Messiah or Christ means to function as the Christ. A functional title is one that is awarded upon the basis of proved performance, such as the title of world's champion heavyweight boxer. Other titles may simply be conferred upon a person regardless of his ability to function previous to the conferring, such as king. Jesus had been the Christ to his followers, and some of them had so recognized him. In their encounter with him, a new possibility of life had presented itself to them, a new self-understanding had become a real possibility.

A new self-understanding is no simple change in life; it represents a radical transformation, a new way of seeing one's whole existence. Religiously, one might say it is conversion. Psychologically, it represents a new identity, a new self. Biblically, we find such a change implied in the metaphor of the new birth and the claim of Christians that they were dead but now are alive. This process of change carries two motifs, judgment and redemption, which are inseparable. In the light of the description of faith given earlier, it will be clear if it is noted here that judgment is the exposing of one's faith as being idolatry. The actual object of one's worship, or faith, is made clear to him and shown to be what it is, not the true and only God, but a fallible, temporal thing, doomed to pass away and hence offering no salvation whatever. In the presence of Jesus, men found their faith candidly, unashamedly exposed. Such an experience is like a dream in which one suddenly discovers that he has left most of his normal wearing apparel at home; he feels profoundly nude, with no place to hide. This is the experience of judgment; it is revelation; it is knowing who and what one is. When Isaiah of old had such an experience, he cried out: " Woe is me! For I am lost; for I am a man of unclean lips, and I dwell in the midst of a people of unclean lips " (Isa. 6:5). The teachings of Jesus, which his life exemplified, pointed out clearly the nature of a life set on God instead of the gods, and by contrast every other kind of life had its shabbiness exposed, its futility revealed.

The first step of judgment alone is not enough, however. One needs more than simply to know of his idolatry. He needs help to reject this self-understanding and to take up a self-understanding before God. More must be said on this subject later; suffice it now to say that Jesus made it possible for those who followed him to put off their old way of life and begin to live by radical trust in God. One begins this new life by accepting himself and his world as they really are, without pretense, sham or idealistic, romantic illusions, accepting them as God's good gifts within which he may find his fulfillment.

The question that must be asked now runs like this: If

one has experienced this kind of judgment upon his idolatry, and has been offered a new way of understanding his life, and *has entered* into this new life of radical trust in the God who brings to naught the gods of this world, what will he say of that which brought him this new possibility? Will he say that it represents the devil? Certainly not! And if he is born into a world in which one's whole way of seeing things is shaped by the heritage of the Old Testament, he will seek to find how to speak of this which has happened to him in terms of that way of seeing the world. It is contended here, on the basis of the evidence developed above, that one who so understands his world will speak of this event as the coming of the Christ to him.

The Christ is the one who presents to us judgment and the possibility of a radical trust in God. This possibility of radical trust is no mere opportunity, but is now in the presence of the Christ a living option, and one must choose it or reject it. The Christians who wrote the New Testament tell us that this is what happened to them in the presence of Jesus. Affirming God in a relationship of trust cannot be understood without realizing that Jesus taught of God in terms of love. In every sense of the word Jesus affirmed with his words and his life that God is trustworthy, indeed that nothing else is really to be trusted. It cannot be affirmed too strongly that Jesus lived the faith that he taught and in fact that his life probably spoke more clearly and profoundly than even his words.

Despite the differences and seeming lacks because of the nationalistic expectations given to the Messianic hopes, those who companied with Jesus found themselves confronted with something that they were driven to understand as the long-expected Messiah. Karl Barth has

penned words that are well suited to express the disciples'
conviction:

" That we have found the Christ in *Jesus of Nazareth* is
confirmed because all the manifestations of God's faithfulness are indications or prophecies of what has encountered us in Jesus. The hidden power of the law and the
prophets is the Christ who encounters us in Jesus. The
meaning of all religion is the redemption, the turn of the
age, the resurrection, the invisibility of God that con-
strains us to silence in Jesus. The substance of all human
happenings is the forgiveness under which they stand as
it is proclaimed and embodied precisely in Jesus. No one
need object that this power, this meaning, this substance
is to be found not only in Jesus but elsewhere. For we ourselves affirm this very thing; indeed, precisely we *can*
affirm it. What is known and found in Jesus is that God is
found everywhere, that before and after Jesus mankind
has been found by God; in him we have the criterion by
which all finding and being found by God may be known
as such and by which we can conceive this finding and
being found as a truth of the eternal order. *Many* walk in
the light of redemption, forgiveness, resurrection; but that
we *see* them walk, that we have eyes for them, we owe
to *one*. In *his* light we see light.

" And that it is *the Christ* we have found in Jesus is confirmed because Jesus is the final word, which clarifies all
the others and brings them to sharpest expression, of the
faithfulness of God to which the law and the prophets
bear witness."[77]

It is here contended that in fact Jesus' very life and
words summoned men to live in radical dependence upon
God's grace, forsaking all other ways of understanding
life, giving up their efforts at self-justification and striving
after glory. In Jesus, men are summoned to hear that they

have not trusted in God and are told that God is the very source of life; distrust of God means shutting oneself off from the very source of life, hence being dead. Furthermore, Jesus presents us with an example of man at one with God, redeemed man. The person of Jesus is the man of faith in God alone.

" According to the biblical picture of Jesus as the Christ, there are, in spite of all tensions, no traces of estrangement between him and God and consequently between him and himself and between him and his world (in its essential nature). The paradoxical character of his being consists in the fact that although he has only finite freedom under the conditions of time and space, he is not estranged from the ground of his being. There are no traces of unbelief. . . . Even in the extreme situation of despair about his messianic work, he cries to his God who has forsaken him. In the same way the biblical picture shows no trace of *hubris* or self-elevation."[78]

Thus Jesus does not only point the way, but walks it. It was this conviction which led the liberal movement to overemphasize Jesus' life as an example. In Tillich's words, Jesus embodies the " New Being."

Jesus is not only the embodiment of a new relationship to God, he is the offering place of that new relationship for all men. The New Testament not only tells us of men who were made new at the hands of Jesus and later by the preaching that grew out of his ministry, but it speaks of him as the " Mercy Seat " (*hilastērion*) (Rom. 3:25), a term taken from the Old Testament and referring to a portion of the Temple. The use of this term is typical of the manner in which New Testament thinkers pulled out Old Testament concepts to describe what they had found in Jesus. The " mercy seat " was the covering of the Ark. Once each year on the Day of Atonement the high priest entered the Holy of Holies, burned incense before the Ark, sprinkled the blood of the sacrifices upon and before the mercy seat, thus making atonement for the sins of himself and the nation in the presence of the covenant law contained in the Ark, and in the presence of Yahweh, whose glory was believed to be peculiarly present at the Ark between the cherubim. The mercy seat thus fittingly symbolizes the place where God and man come together in such a way that right relationships can be established between them.

Jesus summons men to decision about God; his word is the light that makes visible one's true faith and which offers faith in the God who is God. It is fitting, then, that he be called God's Word. That word which was spoken by commandment and prophet now speaks in the form of a life. "Jesus did not bring a new idea; rather in him an old idea ceased being an idea at all and became a living reality. As he talked about the love of God, the love of God itself drew near."[79] Jesus is called the Christ because he is the Christ; in him the judgment and salvation of God are present.

The Symbolic Jesus Christ

In his actual life, Jesus was found to be by his followers a source of a new kind of faith, or perhaps we should say that at his hands a new kind of faith had become a possibility for them. In the presence of Jesus, men experienced judgment and redemption as these have been discussed in the first section of this chapter. This redemptive power did not cease, however, with the end of Jesus' life. The radical trust in God that he had lived and proclaimed as the source of life could still be proclaimed, and it was proclaimed. Because Jesus lived out that new self-understanding, trusting only in God, and in his own being offered it to men, it seemed impossible to speak of the faith apart from its immediate source and exemplification. Jesus Christ became a symbol for the radical trust in God that he proclaimed. To claim him as Lord meant to claim for oneself the relationship to God that had become possible at his hands.

Jesus' disciples knew themselves as men with a commission, to proclaim the love of God that had drawn near in Jesus. It was impossible to make this proclamation apart from the name of the one who had embodied it, it was his gospel and he was the gospel as well. Thus Jesus, who was a material symbol of God's love and his word, the historical man of Nazareth, who was the Christ, became also an abstract symbol. Wherever Jesus Christ is properly preached, men are called to decide for or against God, because their real faith is exposed, revealed, idolatry is shown to be the futile way that it is, and the loving nature of the one who is God is offered. But must we not also be able to put this statement in reverse, that wherever idolatry is shown to be what it is and the loving nature of God is proclaimed, there Jesus Christ is properly preached? Or to put it differently, because we say Jesus is the Christ, must we conclude that the Christ is found only in Jesus?

It is contended here that God has always worked with men as he does in Jesus of Nazareth. " In many and various ways God spoke of old to our fathers by the prophets; but in these last days he has spoken to us by a Son." (Heb. 1:1–2.) " What is known and found in Jesus is that God is found everywhere, that before and after Jesus mankind has been found by God; in him we have the criterion by which all finding and being found by God may be known as such."[80] Or, as found in the Gospel of St. Thomas, " Split a piece of wood—I am there; lift the stone and you will find me there." God has always related himself to his world as its redeemer and always will; this is eternal in the nature of God. There is no other redeemer than God and redemption is always of God. God is sovereign in redemption and in revelation. If by the term "Christ" we mean God's redemptive and revealing activity, then we cannot restrict the term to Jesus of Nazareth, for God made himself known and proclaimed his love long before the history of Jesus.

"It would never have occurred to Paul to doubt that the righteousness of God revealed in Jesus of Nazareth had already long been attested by God's dealing with Israel and thence, as he says, through 'the law and the prophets' (Rom. 3:21). He naturally assumes not only that men universally have the possibility of authentic existence because 'what can be known of God is plain to them' in 'the things that have been made' (Rom. 1:19 f.), but that 'this possibility has especially been given to the Jew through the law, in which he daily encounters God's claim and by which he is daily led to see that he does not exist by and for himself, but that his being is limited by the claim under which he stands.' Paul can also argue in Romans 4 that Abraham is 'the father of us all' and can summon Christians to 'share the faith of Abraham,' not because Abraham believed in Jesus, but because he 'believed God, and it was reckoned to him as righteousness' (vss. 16 and 3)."[81]

Ogden also gives some interesting quotations from F. D. Maurice that make the same point. "Christ *was* before He took human flesh and dwelt among us." "He actually conversed with prophets and patriarchs and made them aware of His presence." He "is in every man, the source of all light that ever visits him, the root of all the righteous thoughts and acts that he is ever able to con-

ceive or do."[82] Such ideas are by no means merely modern.
Calvin asserted in the *Institutes* that we must affirm that
the Jews of the Old Testament knew Christ. Paul plainly
says that the events which called the patriarchs of the
Old Testament to radical trust in God were Christ events.
The rock in the wilderness that gave forth water as the
gift of God, Paul says, was Christ (I Cor. 10:4). And the
New Testament uniformly accepts the Old Testament as
Holy Scripture because it tells of God's speaking to man.

The Christ, then, is God in his revealing redemptive
activity, but for us as Christians, that activity has burst
forth in the historic person Jesus of Nazareth. Jesus has
become for us the normative Christ, the criterion by
which we can recognize contemporary Christ events. A
Christ event is any event that calls man from his anxiety
and self-seeking idolatry to a radical trust in God, for by
definition God has spoken to man through such an event.
Jesus Christ is for Christians the symbol that means judgment and redemption from God himself. The eternal relation of God to man is manifest in Jesus as the Christ.

Jesus Christ became a symbol as the New Testament
disciples reflected upon their faith and its beginning, and
sought to carry out their commission to proclaim God's
love known to them in Jesus. Their reflections made rich
usage of Old Testament figures, especially of those associated with an expected deliverer, a Messiah. The New
Testament is throughout a statement of faith, not an attempt to record "straightforward" newspaper history.
The life of Jesus is told only through the eyes of faith and
is told so as to reveal him as the Christ to the reader.
There is no longer any reason to suppose that we shall be
able to penetrate behind this wall of faith to have for ourselves some sort of literal account of Jesus' life. But what
we do have is what these reporters knew at the deepest

level of their existence to be the truth about themselves and God as it had become known to them in and through Jesus of Nazareth. Historically it is clear that this picture which they have left has the power to transform lives, to create new men of those who are grasped by it. Such power implies that there is an analogy between the picture we have and the reality that is responsible for the changed lives which created the picture. " The symbolic material through which we speak about God is an expression of the divine self-manifestation, and the mediated material which is given to us in the biblical picture of the Christ is the result of the reception of the New Being and its transforming power on the part of the first witnesses."[83]

In this chapter we have discussed the nature of the Christian faith in its relation to Jesus as the Christ; why and how Jesus came to be called the Christ; and how Jesus Christ became a symbolic term. We must turn now to the vexing problem of Biblical interpretation to see how the Christ event recorded can be interpreted so as to lead to faith.

Chapter VII

The Biblical Christ and
the Eternal Christ

AS THE MODERN scientific world view has grown and come to predominate in the mind of mankind during the past three hundred years and more, so the problems of understanding Christianity in any relevant sense have grown apace. It is clear that both the Old Testament and the New Testament were written by people who held a prescientific attitude toward the world. There is no need here to expound on their mythological way of understanding their world, for whatever their way of understanding or "thinking" their world, their actual experience was no less real, no less empirical than ours.[84] It is imperative, however, that the modern Christian learn how to recognize the kinds of experiences about which the Biblical writers were speaking, for only then will he know the relevancy of the Bible for his own existence.

It is no good, of no conceivable value to mankind today, to say that there used to be miracles but that these ended with Bible times, that angels used to speak to men but do so no longer. The logical analysts are correct in regarding such statements as false. Nor can history[85] be of religious meaning[86] to one so long as he is merely objective toward it; it must be allowed to interrogate the affective and conative portion of one's life (as well as the intellectual). This interruption into one's affective and conative life may occur by permission or without it. For example, a letter is received, opened, and read objectively, with acute rationality. But nevertheless, its contents may interrogate one's affective and conative life: an unexpected and fabulous inheritance, the death of a loved one, a lawsuit of great weight against one, an unexpected honor. In any of these cases one is called to rethink himself and his life situation. What does life mean now? How shall it be lived? The past, however, if it is simply treated as matter-of-fact events and met with detached attitude, does not interrogate one's inmost life. In the examples above, one cannot be detached, so that objectivity is not a problem in interpreting history of this kind. The point here is that we must learn also how to interpret past events, viz., those of the Bible, which can be treated quite impersonally and objectively, in such a way that they can interrogate our affective and conative life. Even this latter way of interpretation does not mean that these events *will* become of relevance for the realities of our existence, but no event unless it is so interpreted can become of such relevance.

EXPERIENCE AND ITS INTERPRETATION

The purpose of this chapter is to show *one* way in which our mind-set, our way of putting the question, about Christianity's basic experiential foundations actually precludes their being relevant to human existence, and to suggest a better kind of approach to the Biblical materials. We must first note some things about the ways in which we experience what we do experience and how presuppositions or foreknowledge affect our experiencing.[87] To do this we shall take up some examples well apart from Christianity, neutral, as it were.

Let us first consider a young couple watching an American football game. The boy has seen many games and played in many. The girl, however, has never played in the game, never seen a game, never even heard of such a game. For our purposes we may pretend that so far as *football*, but football only, is concerned she might be a visitor from outer space. The game opens without her having been instructed as to the purpose or " plot " of the game. The kickoff is clean and high, well down the field. It is caught on the twenty-yard line by a fast-running fullback, who streaks off behind three blockers. Quickly he is through the opponents and racing downfield with only the safety man ahead. But escape he cannot; down he comes on the ten-yard line, with five men on top of him.

Now, what have our two people experienced? The young man has seen a brilliant run, a near touchdown. He is thrilled, excited, leaping and shouting. He notices the puzzled look on the girl's face and asks, " What's wrong? " She replies, " What did he do? Why did all those men chase him? Was he trying to steal the ball? " There is no need to belabor the obvious here. The girl has not had at all the same experience as the boy, and the difference has nothing at all to do with the physical facts of the environment. The same phenomenon was interpreted in a totally different context. Neither interpretation can be called *wrong*, but it is clear that the girl's questions were not *appropriate*. Her questions came from a thought framework that did not fit the situation at hand and thus " deformed " or " misappropriated " the phenomenon. It is clear that at least some phenomena, then, can be misappropriated by putting them into an inappropriate framework.

We turn now to a quite different situation, the seeming

conflict between the things that science tells us about ourselves and what we ourselves say. Many times what is said by the scientists is so different from our own firsthand experience that we conclude that one or the other is just plain wrong. We wonder if our world or theirs must go. The physicist, for example, describes a world that is quite foreign to us, a world filled mostly with sheer emptiness in which pulses of energy mass fly about with orderly disorder. All our familiar world of sound, color, warmth, friendship, worry, and joy has vanished. Try as we may, a pulsating electromagnetic wave doesn't quite equal the face of a friend, nor do varying pressure waves in the air seem to be the same thing as the voice of a loved one or a favorite piece of music. Somehow the meaning that our everyday world has for us seems to find no place in the physicists' world. Are we wrong or are the physicists wrong? Are our eyes and ears or our minds fabricating an unreal world? The image in our eyes is inverted on the retina by the passage through the crystalline lens of the eye, but there is no question that we " see " the tree right side up, and try as we may, we see the tree " out there," but cannot see the tree image on our own retina.

Seeing the real tree is no problem, given reasonably normal eyes; the problem arises only when we ask, " How do we see the tree? " with the expectation that we shall find the answer in some internal physicochemical process. We quickly find ourselves in the scientist's world, and our green, friendly, rustling shade tree has somehow vanished. We have only physical and chemical processes.

Certainly there is nothing improper about investigating sight, but the questions: " How do we see? " and " What takes place in us when we see trees? " are inappropriate if what we want to know is, " Can I or can I not see trees? " or, " Do I or do I not see a tree? " Those questions are to be asked of the viewer, not the psychologist and physiologist, and the viewer does not need their help to answer. Seeing the tree is not the end product of a physiological chain reaction any more than is winning a footrace.[88] Winning footraces, or losing them for that matter, is not a discoverable physiological process because it is not a physiological process at all, though physiological processes take place and may be studied. Seeing or hearing likewise are not physiological processes. This fact is perfectly clear now if we think back to the example of the couple at the football game and what they "saw."

We now have before us three important points about experience: first, past experience, history, is only meaningful in a religious sense, i.e., becomes of weight for one's faith, if it is so interpreted as to be capable of interrupting the affective and conative portion of one's life as well as the intellectual, for man is a unity of all these aspects. Second, phenomena can be misappropriated by putting them into an inappropriate framework. Third, some parts of experience cannot be suitably explained by the scientific framework as such, and may even disappear in that context.

SOME NEW PRINCIPLES FOR BIBLICAL INTERPRETATION

We turn now to consider one particular facet of Christian experience, one that is of central importance and one that is a source of many problems for Christians today. These problems arise in the main because the New Testament writers speak of experiencing the Christ (for the moment, suffice it to say that we mean the post-Easter Christ) in at least quasi-physical terms. Further, it is common to interpret these experiences as something which happened then, but cannot in principle be repeated in our own experience, thus making it necessary to show some other way they can be meaningful in the present. One orthodox procedure at this point is to make these New Testament descriptions evidences for the God-man nature of Jesus. It must be doubted that this procedure succeeds in allowing the Biblical experience access to one's affective and conative life. Can it do more than lead one to say that something *was true*, i.e., give simple rational assent to a past fact? Is it not merely the acceptance of a conclusion based on sufficient reason? It is certainly clear that this assent is not what is meant by faith in the sense used in this book. For, as we have seen earlier, faith is the *actual central concern* of one's life; it is the "religion" by which one really lives. It seems obvious that one cannot actually *live* by mere rational assent to a past fact of history as a purely past fact. Because mere rational assent means an objective "So what?" attitude, the contention here is that mere rational assent to a past fact allows one to turn away from history empty and unchallenged. If, however, the past facts have implications about *all* of history and particularly about *my* history, then I may be challenged as to my understanding of my own history, my own existence. One lives his life on the basis of his understanding of his own existence. It seems doubtful that metaphysical dogmas offer much challenge to contemporary human self-understanding, for rational assent to dogma does not appear to involve the affective and conative aspects of man. As someone has said, it is unheard of that one would die for the sake of the ontological argument for the existence of God. The orthodox procedure appears to create as many problems as it solves. Its error is like that of the girl at the football game; it is putting the New Testament experiences into an inappropriate framework, in this case using them to support metaphysical dogmas.

If these New Testament experiences are to become meaningful, they must be understood as experiences that are not "merely historical" and past, but are in some way at least analogous to potential or actual human experience today.[89] The past, in the sense of events over and done with, is the subject matter of the science of history as it is ordinarily practiced. The orthodox approach to the New Testament experiences in question is similar in some respects to the approach of scientific history.[90] Now, just as physics and physiology are inappropriate for interpreting the meaning of such an experience as hearing a symphony or winning a footrace, so the science of history is inappropriate for interpreting religious experiences. When its canons are applied, even if inadvertently or unintentionally, certain kinds of experiences are either misappropriated or not appropriated at all. It is not concerned with meanings, but with happenings. It assigns meanings to the category of the "subjective" and treats them as secondary phenomena, just as physics does color experience. Further, history could not exist as a science unless it did so. However, it is the meaning of these New Testament experiences that is the concern of the religious inquiry and for it, meaning is the primary not the secondary phenomenon, just as for the runner, it is winning the race that is the primary phenomenon, not his physiological processes. The scientific historical approach can no more discover the Christ than can the physiological approach discover the winner of the footrace.

Is there some approach that can relieve these problems? There is if we can clear from ourselves the feeling that our primary concern is to "discover" the objective facts of the past, to find out what really happened. The answer will mean that the findings of scientific historical investigation are to be treated as of only secondary value to the religious inquiry. To say that the findings of scientific history are of secondary value does not mean that they must be considered only after the religious meaning is settled. The situation is akin to that of physics in which the sensory perception of color is considered secondary and yet without it there would have been no talk of visible light and no scientific investigation of it. In this fashion the secondary phenomenon is the generating and prior one. Scientific history and textual history, the critical evaluation of tradition and Scripture, represents the sensory perception, though obviously not a literal description as we would describe objective experience in the ordinary sense. Even if scientific history should state that we are dealing with a pious fraud, there is still open a possibility of religious meaning, but that fact will now be a part of the interpretation and may well change its meaning radically.

Certain interpretative principles can now be suggested: (1) The work of the scientific historian (or critical Biblical scholar) will be done first. Whatever objective facts can be known, and certainly the best text available, are definitely to be used. There is at no point to be a *sacrificium intellectus* before the Biblical account; reason does not need to be dissolved to make room for faith. As Jaspers writes, " Reason urges us to leave nothing out of account, to relate ourselves to everything that is, to seek beyond all limits what is and should be, to encompass even antinomies, and always apprehend the whole, to apprehend every possible harmony."[91] Or again, reason "presses toward the One that is all, it does away with the delusion that fixates the One that is all, it does away with the delusion that fixates the One prematurely, incompletely, in partisanship."[92] Thus reason, in fact, is not opposed to anything but a false faith, a faith that " fixates the One prematurely." Reason, however, goes far beyond scientific history, for it insists that personal and collective experience of every type and level be given its own proper voice.

(2) Interpretation will take as its basic premise that the Biblical materials, whenever they can be interpreted meaningfully, will speak to the interpreter about present human existence. The possibility must be left open that not all the Biblical materials will be meaningful, at least to a given interpreter. This point does not import an artificial standard by which to judge Scripture, but does recognize that interpretation cannot proceed responsibly (if indeed at all) unless the interpreter hears what Scripture has to say and hears it with *understanding*. The point to be made is that understanding a text is an endeavor which always is undertaken from some specific perspective. The interpreter questions the text on the basis of his own life situation. Further, the text cannot speak to him about experience that is utterly outside his ken, or logically contradictory, such as square circles. As Bultmann puts it: " The forces that are effective in connecting phenomena are understandable only if the phenomena themselves that are thereby connected are also understood! This means that an understanding of the subject matter itself belongs to historical understanding."[93] One cannot understand, it seems, recorded human experience unless he understands, at least in a provisional or preliminary way, the potentialities of being human about which the text speaks. Scripture, it is contended, intends to be a message calling man from sin to faith in God, and not primarily a report about certain events that have happened. To understand this call, one must have some foreknowledge, even if in an unconscious way, of the life of sin and of faith in God.

(3) Interpretation will accept and use critically the insight that Biblical materials vary in manner of writing

from virtually intentional historical description to fully mythological accounts. Yet the presumed intention is to point to the religious meaning[94] of human experience. In every case the religious inquiry will probe into the Scriptural account with a view to disclosing this deeper meaning, which may be more or less "hidden." Such probing cannot be done without involvement. As Bultmann phrases it, "Real understanding would, therefore, be paying heed to the question posed in the work which is to be interpreted, to the claim which confronts one in the work."[95] Or as Graf Yorck said, "The reality of history does not become visible at all for the spectator who is not personally involved in it."[96]

How Paul Met Christ

Let us see, then, in what way we can talk about meeting the Christ that will be appropriate and allow such a New Testament experience to become a matter of affective and conative concern for us. First, we shall declare what should now be obvious, that it is a mistake to talk about meeting Christ as if this were some physical fact which can be objectively established. Taking Paul's experience on the Damascus road as our Biblical base, we will attempt to show that it is a mistake, an inappropriate interpretation, to speak of this as some kind of visual or auditory experience brought about by a physically objective stimulus. Everyone realizes that there is no point in asking how fast Paul was traveling toward Damascus, and few would think it anything but foolish to ask what color the flash of light was that apparently blinded him. Surprisingly enough, however, almost everyone tries to interpret this passage as if it were talking about an experience of light and sound either caused by external stimulus, or of a hallucinatory nature. These approaches are as misguided and fruitless as probing a Shakespearean play by asking about its mass and velocity, or searching for some real graveyard in which Romeo and Juliet are buried. Or as if my friend should ask me, when I tell him that I have seen the light on some moral issue, how bright it was and what kind of spectacles I wore to see it. Meeting the Christ is an experience more akin to this moral kind of seeing the light than to any ordinary sensory experience.

The Biblical accounts of Paul's experience are baffling if approached only from the scientific historical viewpoint. According to Acts, ch. 9, Paul was blinded by a light from heaven and heard a Voice; the men around him heard the Voice but saw no one. Later in Damascus, Paul was commissioned to go to the Gentiles with the gospel. According to Acts, ch. 22, Paul was blinded due to the brightness of a light from heaven and he heard a voice; the men with him saw the light but did not hear the Voice, a reversal of Acts, ch. 9. As before, Paul at Damascus received his sight and was commissioned to go to the Gentiles. According to Acts, ch. 26, Paul saw a bright light and heard a Voice, but no blindness is mentioned here. However, Paul was commissioned on the spot to go to the Gentiles and it was the Gentiles who were to have their eyes opened that they might " turn from darkness to light." In Gal., ch. 1, neither light, Voice, nor blindness is mentioned, only the commission to the Gentiles.

What can we conclude from the considerable difference in these three accounts in The Acts written by the same man to tell about the same event? Can we seriously maintain that Luke was at all concerned to record what " objectively " happened? It is apparent that any attempt to " reconcile " these accounts and gain the scientific historical truth is doomed to failure because the author himself was incredibly careless about what "objectively" happened. His entire way of recording this event for posterity is designed to point to the religious import of the event. In terms of scientific history, all that can be said, and indeed all that needs to be said, is that Luke purports to be telling about a religious experience of the apostle Paul. (Obviously, some other things, such as approximate time and place, could also be conjectured.) We must conclude that Luke used the light and Voice from heaven, and the blindness, to speak of what might be termed "inner" experiences and states in Paul.

The light and Voice from heaven mean first, that Paul, and the others as well, believed that what he experienced was not hallucinatory or merely psychological. His experience originated at the instance of God; it was an encounter, not a self-induced experience; it came without warning and without conscious choosing. We should probably understand that Luke identifies Word and Light in much the same manner that John does. God's Word and his Light are one and the same. Their function is to reveal one's inmost state and direct one to the source of genuine fulfillment. First, one's inmost state, his real faith, is made to stand out and thereby be revealed for what it is. One is shown that, and how he has been fleeing from the limitations of being finite and the responsibilities of being a self. The way of one's flight into the world of things and deeds or ideas is brought home in all its fearfulness. Then, and only if the first flash of light is accepted, only if the Word finds hearing ears, a new possibility is opened; a new possibility that is also an old and previously rejected possibility, namely, that the limitations of being finite be accepted and affirmed, and the responsibilities of being a self be taken up. This new possibility is characterized by freedom and responsibility, by genuine selfhood. One is freed from his flight and from the slavery to the world that went with it. The uses of words, things, and deeds are now seen to be for the exercise of one's responsible selfhood within the accepted limitations of being finite. The finite self in this way is no longer lost, but affirmed in its relationship to the world.

Does this interpretation above fit the pattern of Paul's life? Previous to this Damascus road experience, he had, he tells us, been a Pharisee of the Pharisees, and at the moment saw his life being fulfilled by his efforts to stamp out the followers of the Way. His life was *spent* in obedience to the law and now in the obliteration of the opponents of Judaism. The Word comes to Paul that all this is merely kicking against the goad, and in fact hurting himself. This Word from heaven is identified with Jesus, and the persecution is said to be directed against him, presumably against the gospel he preached and lived.

At this point Paul is informed that all this is not the purpose of life, another purpose is to be made known to him (Acts, ch. 26). Apparently, before this purpose can be known, the judgment imposed must be accepted. But the acceptance of this judgment means nothing less than dying to a whole way of life. Paul must see that his understanding of the meaning and ground of his life hitherto has been a false way, a fleeing way, an escape from God, not an approach to him. The light from heaven enables Paul to know, that, although he has eyes, he does not see; he is one of the blind sons of Israel. His way of life is a blind way of life. As Luke tells the story, Paul, like Jonah, is to be three days and three nights in darkness, and without food or drink before the proper mission of his life can begin. Also, as with Jonah, that mission is to begin in a great Gentile city. Paul sees that his blind way of life is actually a flight from his own life; he is hurting himself, not helping God; the way of the Pharisee is a rebellion against God. It falsely elevates the Jew and falsely cuts off the Gentile. " None is righteous, no, not one; no one understands, no one seeks for God. . . . There is no fear of God before their eyes." (Rom. 3:10,18.) Only when Paul is obedient to this revelation does a new possibility open itself, namely, that he shall live as one who knows the depth of his own sin, and one who can have his blindness healed by those whom he has persecuted. Had he been disobedient to the heavenly vision, it would have been for him no heavenly vision, i.e., he would have denied its heavenly origin, its validity as truth about him.

In accepting himself as one who is blind and in consenting to be told the meaning of life by the disciples in Damascus, Paul opens himself to life. He is freed from his flight, freed from slavery to the Pharisaic way. Only now is there possibility that his words and deeds can be an expression of responsible selfhood, previously they expressed only slavery to the Pharisaic world. The emergence of this genuine selfhood is symbolized in the Biblical accounts by the change of name from Saul to Paul.

Only the new self can be called to love of neighbor in any responsible way. For Paul, love of neighbor was to be a proclaiming of the love of God for Jew and Gentile without distinction. To the Jew, this message must come as a scandal, and to the Gentile as foolishness, but in each case, a denial of his own particular faith. The scandal to the Jew is the denial that God is the God of the Jews any more than of the Gentiles. The foolishness to the Gentiles is that only he who loses his life will save it and that man needs forgiveness for his best deeds along with his worst.

What is clear from the Biblical accounts concerning Paul's Damascus road experience is that Paul's understanding of God and of himself was radically altered at just this time. He experienced judgment on his whole way of life and his understanding of it. His religious understanding was put under the light of God, shown to be wrong, and he was offered a new understanding.

Meeting the Christ is, then, to experience being judged and enlightened, to have one's religious understanding called into question, and to be offered a new understanding. Religious understanding here means nothing less than the religion by which one actually lives; that understanding of life by which one sees the purpose of his life; that understanding of what life is all about which makes him who and what he is in the way he is. When this heart of one's life is called into question, judged, and enlightened, when one is offered a new understanding of life, then one is meeting the Christ. Presumably, this kind of experience is potentially at hand in the daily encounters of life, but it is so emotionally demanding that we learn to evade these encounters. No one likes to have the very meaning of his life put into question, even occasionally. So we learn to live most of our lives with our religious understanding pushed below the level of awareness, manifesting itself only in our moods, e.g., joy, sadness, fear, anxiety.

Does approaching the experience of meeting the Christ in the way suggested above, then, allow this experience to have entrance to our affective and conative life? It seems, certainly, to show that the apparent confusion in the Biblical accounts of Paul's experience are concerning matters of scientific historical fact that are of no weight for our religious approach and were of no weight, obviously, to the writer Luke. In fact, asking, "What really happened?" by looking for the "facts," turns us aside from the religious import of these accounts. What hap-

pened in physical fact is apparently not described, but
what happened in Paul's religious understanding is our
prime material of Christian experience. The scientific historical approach can in fact be a way to escape from
having one's life put in question; it keeps the Christ
experience safely in the past. So also is the orthodox approach a way of escape by pronouncing "miracle" over
these historical facts and then turning to worship the
miracle itself by giving it intellectual assent, a procedure
that takes little or no emotional involvement and demands
no change in life. Any approach is clearly inappropriate
that allows one to take up an objective, almost impartial,
attitude, for it allows one to avoid the encounter with the
religious situation of his own life.

Having seen Paul's experience of the Christ as encounter that transcends the ordinary objective encounters
of life, but which cannot be separated out as another
variety of such encounter, we can now, at least, be freed
from trying to make the Christ a part of the scientific,
empirical world. The Christ, as God in his relationship to
the world, transcends the subjective and objective categories and hence cannot become an object. Paul, in this
experience we have discussed, became aware that the
Christ was present for him in Jesus of Nazareth. This is
probably most simply stated by saying that Paul now
became aware that the word of God for him was truly
present in the ministry and preaching of Jesus. This need
not imply the kind of metaphysical identity between God
and Jesus which the later creeds employed. The metaphysical concepts of the ancient church have lost their
meaning for us. In fact, our interpretation of them is
usually accomplished by translating them unconsciously
into the subject-object categories of the modern world
view. This process is not merely misleading, but in fact

obscures the meaning of the incarnation as God factually then and now making his grace available to us in Jesus Christ, and it further tends to objectify God. The nature of the unity of God and Jesus Christ is best understood historically, not metaphysically.[97]

The presence of the Christ for Paul meant the condemnation of his previous understanding of the relation of God, world, and self. If the Pharisaic-Judaistic way and the Gentile way alike are under condemnation, what way is left? If all human understanding is under the curse of sin, how can a man think his way out? The answer must be that there is no way out for human endeavor! The priority of initiative belongs to God. The word of Jesus here is that God has always already drawn nigh; his Kingship is at hand for Jew and Gentile alike; repent (of your self-striving) and receive these joyous tidings. Then go and tell your neighbor.

Having seen the experience of Paul in this light, we can now have our own affective and conative life gripped. How are we living, like Jew or Gentile? Is our God some part of the empirical world? Is our hope for meaning in science, or the welfare state, or personal accomplishment? If questions like these arise to plague us, we may suspect that the eternal Christ is meeting us too, here and now, as we read these lines, calling to us to acknowledge that "Our redemption is no longer a question of pursuit but of surrender to Him who is always and everywhere present."[98]

Chapter VIII

Theology, Education, and Ministry

IT HAS BECOME increasingly hard to see any clear separation between the practice of most churches and the "American way of life." The preceding chapters have suggested the ways in which the nature of faith is misunderstood: faith and Christian faith are confused; God is not distinguished from the gods; his redemptive activity is not related to the anxiety resulting from the death of the idols, but is restricted to the preaching of dogma, moralism, and the historical Jesus of Nazareth. The contention is that these theological confusions and errors can be traced to a practice of ministry and theology which has encouraged widespread use of unexamined symbolic expressions, the meaning of which has become less and less clear. Words have been given supremacy over meaning. Certain words are set apart as holy and necessary and are used as if automatically meaningful. Such action ignores the real purpose of language, which is to communicate. The words are not the important factor; the message that the words actually bear from speaker to hearer is the important factor. Words are only carriers, they are not the message. The message that words bear can be determined only by an examination of the total context within which such words are spoken and heard.

It seems clear that the New Testament writers did not

limit themselves to one narrow range of symbols. The earliest preaching seems most dependent upon certain aspects of the Jewish sacrificial rites for its conceptual framework. From this source came the description of Jesus as the lamb of God, sacrificed for the sin of the world. The apostle Paul soon discovered that such Jewish symbolism did not tell non-Jewish people about the Christ who called them from the gods to God. He seized upon a current religious mythology, Gnosticism, which was understood by the people to whom he was speaking, and used it as a conceptual framework within which to present his message. His message, however, was certainly not Gnosticism, but rather the end of Gnosticism. From this source came the description of Jesus as the heavenly being who put off his godly garb to descend to earth as man for the redemption of man. Still later, the Gospel of John finds it necessary or useful to make certain alterations in both these previous conceptual frameworks. Instead of the heavenly being, it is God's Word, the creative and redemptive activity of God, that has been and always will be the true light that enlightens every man; that Word it is which became flesh. It is apparent that the New Testament writers felt it possible and advisable to alter their chosen conceptuality to bear the message that they wanted it to bear to a particular audience. They did not equate the gospel with any particular conceptual presentation of it.

The confusion about the meaning of faith and Christian faith has allowed a shift in emphasis from meaning to words. This shift is most easily seen in those cases where faith is equated with intellectual affirmation of dogma. If the correctness of the dogma to be believed is the most important factor, then words are paramount. Further, it becomes necessary to forget that language is dynamic and contextual because then any given expression would be merely relative and there could be no truly orthodox expressions. Such a transformation of faith into the believing of correct dogma is psychologically desirable because it gives one a sense of security. It further makes it appear that one is not himself ultimately responsible for believing what he does believe; it is the authorities who are responsible.

Similar analogies can be made about each of the distortions of faith, for none of them lay claim to the total person. In each case they are ways of being less than totally responsible for one's own life before the only god who is God. Christian faith means nothing less than to live responsibly by one's trust in that final one who is God, known in Christian terms as the God and Father of our Lord Jesus Christ. The goal of Christianity is that every person may actually live his life responsibly by his trust in this God. It is this emphasis on faith as involving the whole person in a self-conscious, responsible way which makes it totally unacceptable to substitute words for meanings and thus permit the use of unexamined symbols as if their meaning were inseparably attached to the symbols themselves. If faith in the Christian sense is a responsible act stemming from one's encounters with the Christ event in his own life, and representing a turning from faith in idols to faith in God, it is urgent that the communications of the church be such as to identify the contemporary work of the Christ, describe contemporary idolatry, and call people to faith in the God of Christianity by explaining what all these mean, using symbols that are effective for modern man. We have attempted in earlier chapters to make this explanation in a preliminary way.

A knowledge of the theology of these previous chapters is presumed in the following discussion in which we ask what this all means for the professional ministry of the church today. In a sentence, it means that the professional ministry will no longer be able to understand itself as primarily a preaching, pastoral, and sacramental ministry, but will have to become primarily and self-consciously a theological-educational ministry. Such a ministry implies a new relationship between the professional ministry of the church and the work of those specialists whom we now usually find teaching in our seminaries, as well as to the laity of the church. There must once and for all be an end to any understanding that permits the professional ministry to think of its task as enlisting the laity to assist in protecting and perpetuating the organized church, rather than conceiving the professional ministry as help-meets to the laity, to whom is entrusted the task of proclaiming the gospel in the world.

Part of the cause for the failure of today's professional ministry to be of assistance to the laity in its task of ministry is due to its failure to conceive of its task as essentially theological and educational. Theology as a task has been assigned to professional theologians and education to professional educators. Underlying this understanding of the professional ministry is the traditional division of theology into exegetics, systematics, and practics. This tripartite division presupposes that the "path" the gospel takes from God to man follows a certain route; it begins with God's inspiring the Bible writers and ends with a proclaiming of the Biblical message in Biblical words. Systematic theology, occupying a central position, sets the tone for the whole, and the systematic theologian dominates the whole process. Communication proceeds in one direction only. The practice of preaching in the usual Sunday church service typifies this one-way communication process. Unexpressed, but implied in such a scheme is the thought that only exegetical and systematic scholars are in a position really to originate information, and that their information comes strictly from Biblical sources.

It is certainly correct that Christianity is Biblically oriented and that a continuing relation to the Bible is essential to Christianity. Biblical exegesis is and will continue to be an important aspect of the total theological enterprise of the church. If one believes, however, that God is living and active, that the Holy Spirit moves the hearts of men today, as most Christian thought contends, then theology is more than Biblical theology. There are two foundations for theology: the Biblical expressions of faith and the witness of the Spirit in the heart of man. Whatever canon of truth there can be for theological expressions must take into consideration these two foundations and not permit either to dominate alone. The Biblical basis for theology is dependent upon the process of exegesis, which can and does err. The expressions of the witness of the Spirit, on the other hand, may be deformed by the desires of men or councils. Any useful process for theology must concern itself with the congruence of the two foundations. Both exegesis and the testimony of the Spirit are necessary. Theology is a task of the whole church, not any one part of it, for it is certain to Protestants that God does not particularly give his inspiration to scholars or councils as such, but to the whole church. Some must lead, of course, but a living theology will have to be forged in dialogue with God's people.

Some formal means needs to be established for communication to be other than one-way; the preachers, teachers, theologians, and exegetes need an ear to hear what the Spirit says to God's people. If there is not communication in both directions, the Protestant Church is as autocratic and hierarchical as it usually accuses the Roman Catholic Church of being, and the "priesthood of all believers" is a joke as far as the laity is concerned. The "priesthood of all believers" implies a conviction that God does indeed give his Spirit to his people and the Protestant theologian must, above all, demonstrate some faith in this conviction or deny his own theology.

Perhaps, in the past, it was necessary for the major part of the task of theology to be done by the scholars and handed on as a completed body of divinity to the laity of the church. This *may* have been necessary, and if so, was justified only because of the general lack of education of believers, which would make it virtually impossible for them to express their faith adequately in a conceptual way. It can further be justified in that there was, until the past hundred years or more, a reasonably unified conceptual framework within which to speak. Today the situation is vastly different. Education, especially in the United States, is offered to many more people at a much higher level than at any other time or place in the history of man. The conceptual framework, or universe of discourse, is not a unified one, but in the United States is probably dominated by the scientific world view. For these reasons, our problem is quite different from that of a century ago, and radically different from the situation faced by Luther or Calvin.

There are many phrases in common use to describe contemporary man which seek to suggest the way in which man today differs from man in all previous history. Some speak of twentieth-century man, others of the new man, or the new mankind; Bonhoeffer spoke of man come of age or the world come of age, and Tillich speaks of autonomous man who is insecure in his autonomy. However one denominates man today, there is general agreement that he is in some significant way different from his ancestors. This difference is best suggested in the concepts " adulthood " and " autonomy " because they imply self-direction and responsibility. Man believes that he is responsible for himself and his world in a way that he never believed before. This belief in autonomy is not brought about so much by the scientific developments which allow him control of the world as it is by the attitude toward his world that the scientific world view, added upon the Christian understanding of man as the gardener of the world, has brought.

Man cannot now think of himself and his world as pawns under the dominion of vying supernatural powers. Man does not believe himself at the mercy of demons or devils unseen and uncontrollable. He cannot view destiny as a foreordained end. For good or ill, man today views the world as pluralistic and open-ended. He is not usually so foolish that he thinks all factors are now or ever will be under his control, but he sees this lack of control to be a product of the sheer complexity of all large processes, not a case of causal control by higher powers than his own. Man thinks of himself as autonomous in that he now assumes history to be his province; he is the maker of history, not merely its subject and observer. And though he is to some extent a captive of history, having his own givenness, he regards the future as in principle open, i.e., subject to modification by his own actions in the here-and-now. Such an attitude toward history represents a fundamental change in man. He must now bear burdens unthinkable to his immediate ancestors.

Because man has come of age, man the believer has come of age too, and the professionals must no longer do his theologizing for him. It is now necessary to involve the people of the local church in the task of theology to the maximum degree possible in order that they may be truly the ministry of the church that God has called them to be. It is clear that the exegetical and systematic theologian cannot perform the task of involving the people of the church in theology. For the new man, exegetical theology will perform largely the task it has always performed, but it must also be prepared to hear and attend to what man, the believer, is saying. The systematic theologian can no longer perform his role in entirely the same way; it is no longer possible that any one theologian will write *the* theology for a great mass of humanity as did Luther or Calvin. What systematic theology can do for the new man is to offer various conceptual systems for the understanding of Christian faith that can then be tried out in the local congregation, modified, experimented with, and the results returned to the systematic theologian for refinement.

The work that is to be performed by a professional ministry for the laity in such a new kind of theological situation can hardly be carried out by a sacramental or preaching ministry in the usual sense of these. The preaching ministry of today cannot possibly do what preaching did in historic Protestantism. It cannot do so because the people have changed and the place that preaching plays in the life of the average person has changed. During the first three centuries of Protestantism, the sermon was a major element in terms of education and influence in the life of the faithful. Not only was the minister usually the best educated man of the community, but the church exercised great power. Even then, however, the sermon was never assumed to be sufficient for training the laity; the pastoral visit, for example, had an instructional motive.

Finally, modern knowledge has cast grave doubt upon

the effectiveness of any communication that proceeds, as the sermon does, in one direction only. One-way communication is inefficient as a message carrier and often leaves grave misunderstandings. It is particularly inadequate when difficult or unfamiliar ideas are to be used or explained.

If this seems dubious to you, try this little experiment on some friends. Draw five rectangles of the same size, connected together in varying ways. As a first experiment have someone try to tell the others how to draw these figures on a sheet of paper. In this case the leader must not face the group, show them the drawing, make any gestures or answer any questions in any way, nor are the group to talk among themselves, or let others see the drawings they are making. The leader is to stop when he thinks he has given enough information.

As a second step in the experiment, allow another person to be the leader and use a slight variation on the first drawing. This leader may face the group and answer any questions, but may not show the drawing, nor make any gestures to describe it, nor ask any questions; group and leader must use only words.

As the third step in the experiment, allow still another person to be the leader. This leader may do all that the second leader was permitted, but also may ask questions and may see the drawings the group are making, although he may not show his own drawing or use any gesture; again the only communication is verbal.

The time required for each step should be noted, the accuracy of results estimated, and both group and leader asked about their feelings at the end of each. In the first experiment, usually, the results will be something like this: The time taken will be shortest, the accomplished results very poor, but the leader will have felt that he was doing a good job and the group will have felt frustrated and irritated by the leader's seeming incompetence. The time taken for the second phase will be longer than that for the first, the results much better, and in this case the leader will have felt frustrated, and perhaps even threatened, but the group will have been more satisfied with him. In the third phase of the experiment, the time will be as long or longer than the second, the drawings of the group still more accurate, and both group and leader more satisfied with each other than in either of the first two steps.

One-way communication is totally inadequate for most kinds of educational effort, and the kind of work that needs to be done by the professional ministry today is best described as theological-educational. This work demands knowledge of and skill in the teaching-learning process. The discipline of Christian education has traditionally concerned itself with teaching and learning, but has not conceived its task in any significant sense to include the sharing of the endeavors of the systematic and exegetical scholars. For this reason perhaps, along with some suggested earlier, the Christian educator has done little to alleviate the theological and Biblical ignorance of the average layman. If any future professional ministry must have this theological-educational center, then all who train for work in the church's professional ministry will have to be proficient in theological *and* educational matters. Any future Christian education of worth must accept as part of its role the sharing of the work of the exegetical and systematic scholars. This will be a new role for Christian education; let us examine what it is and how it can be performed.

The task of Christian education is, in general terms, nothing less than the task committed to the whole church, viz., to be ambassador for Christ in word and deed. Its distinction from the other branches of theology is not in the overall task to which all are committed equally, but in the particular focus of Christian education upon the "nurture" of people both inside and outside the visible church. Nurture, in simple terms, is the encouraging of faith in God, the life of faith in God, and the understanding of these, through intellectual, affective, and conative *teaching* and *learning*. All these avenues of teaching must be used because faith includes them all, as we have observed earlier, in its nature as the centering act of the total personality.

Because it must deal in detail with the teaching-learning process, Christian education is vitally concerned with the meanings of words and word systems for people in varying contexts. This concern means that Christian education is as much involved in hermeneutics as is systematic theology or exegetic theology. In much recent theology, hermeneutics is still interpreted as a one-way process: the proclamation of "saving facts." Heinrich Ott has correctly labeled this kind of hermeneutics as empty-headed thoughtlessness; it is so because it fails to understand either the nature of Christian faith or the nature of man, and totally neglects the *hearing* aspect of communicating the gospel.

Such thinking about hermeneutics fails to do justice to the nature of the gospel, to the nature of the church, and to the nature of language. It misses the nature of the church as a body constituted solely by *faith* in God. The faith of the church is not faith in a body of dogma, but is a relationship to God. A Biblicistic or *Heilsgeschichte* theology fails to grasp this existential nature of the church because it tends to equate faith with intellectual assent to certain "saving facts." In such thinking, the gospel is equated with the "saving facts" about certain historical, long-past events. Faith, in this context, means believing that these events took place as described. Again the existential nature of faith in God is missed.

Faith in God as the centering act of personality is the dynamic of one's life. As we have seen, one always must be concerned about his existence and thus always understands himself in some way. Faith in God seeks to express itself both in words and deeds and to understand itself, to explain itself to itself. As faith in God seeks to express itself in words and to understand itself, the problems of the nature of language and its relation to the people who use and hear it are of extreme significance. Man is the user of symbols who tells himself who he is by his symbols. The symbols that he uses do not mean the same thing in every context, however. As a minimum, the context that determines the meaning of any given symbol includes the personal history of the hearer, plus the psychological and sociological situation affecting the symbol and the communications context.

A Biblicistic or *Heilsgeschichte* view of theology fails to come to grips with the problems of language in connection with the gospel because it assumes that an appropriate language, the meaning of which is fixed and clear, is given, or even prescribed, in the Bible or in confessional formulas. The problem of meaning is avoided by asserting that man's understanding cannot, in principle, be a criterion for the word of God. Such a view will not do at all. The problem of language and the hearer must be faced clearly. This issue cannot be ignored because theology itself will not permit it; the nature of the gospel will not permit it.

God wills that all men should come to faith in him and to this end has ordained the gospel and given it a place in the history of man that is passed from generation to generation by means of understanding. If the gospel is in some way communicable, it must basically be intelligible, understandable. If it is intended for all mankind, then it must be basically understandable by all. The gospel itself is understandable, thus the meaning of the language that purports to convey the gospel must be examined in the context in which it is used. The church must exercise due care that any failure of the world to hear or heed the gospel is not due to the fact that the church has failed to speak understandably. Language is a tool. Whether or not a given series of symbols conveys the gospel is a question to be asked of the hearer in dialogue with the speaker; it cannot be predetermined by the speaker. Attacking the problem of language and the hearer is a manifold task involving several distinct disciplines focusing on this one task—how to speak the gospel meaningfully by word and deed so as to be heard and understood. It is not a complete block to communication to be like Lewis Carroll's Humpty Dumpty, who said, "When *I* use a word, it means just what I choose it to mean— neither more nor less" if one, like Humpty Dumpty, is willing and prepared to explain with *other* words what he has meant by these. Nonetheless, one cannot either demand or expect that his symbols mean what they do not mean in the lives of others. Christian education must be concerned to find out what symbols are *alive* in the world today to see whether they can be used in the communication process that attempts to make Christian faith understandable.

The scholarly task of Christian education centers in the study of the communication and the communication process that attempts to make Christian faith understandable both to those who have this faith and to those who do not. This study is elaborated into several disciplines or fields, but all of them are of concern because they contribute to understanding and utilizing the above kind of communication. Communication is not limited to words, nor are teaching and learning limited to verbal situations, hence this study is not limited to verbal processes. Exemplary of the processes involved are the following: (1) Symbols and the place they play in self-understanding, particularly in Christian self-understanding. (2) The psychosociological situation in which communication takes place, for example, the nature of the group, the communication networks and arrangements, the human relations involved, the physical environment. (3) The personal or psychological situation of teacher and hearer and probable effects of their interaction under varying situations of emotion, age, education, mental ability, and intellectual content of material. (4) The particular situation of linguistic usage and history, i.e., the local symbolic environment. (5) Communications aids, i.e., language supplements and art forms. (6) Nonverbal communication theory and usage.

As a preliminary to its own studies, Christian education must ground itself in the disciplines of exegetical and systematic theology and of philosophy; these provide the basis on which its own efforts can take place. Without the grounding in exegetical and systematic theology, Christian education cannot relate the content of the Christian faith in its historical manifestations to the communication problem. Neglecting these would in effect be creating a one-way hermeneutics in reverse from that described above. This latter error has in fact been prevalent in much religious education insofar as it has emphasized religious experience in a pietistic and uncritical manner that has led to identifying Christian faith with some particular kinds of emotions and moral behavior. Against this it must be said again that there are two foundations for testing expressions of Christian faith; the one, Biblical expressions of faith and elaborations of these in the history of the church; the other, the contemporary witness of the Spirit in the heart of man to the contemporary Christ. Without the grounding in philosophy, particularly ontology and logical analysis, Christian education will probably fail to have an appropriate grasp of its own methodology and language.

The discipline of Christian education cannot be carried on in isolation from the local church and its theological-educational ministry. Part of the task of this discipline is to hear the response to attempts at communication. Only in the church and in the world outside of the theological seminary is it possible to find out whether or not communication is taking place with understanding. Thus the completion of Christian education involves doing that about which it theorizes. This procedure implies some kind of evaluative criteria and procedure. The cue for such evaluative criteria is the purpose of the communication situation, i.e., to make Christian faith understandable both to those who have this faith and to those who do not. If the attainment of this goal is facilitated, then the communications efforts are fruitful.

We can begin to see now why and how it is that theology as a task must be carried out by the whole church. Theology is the search for a conceptual linguistic framework that is appropriate and effective for the explication of Christian faith, i.e., for that living faith which characterizes those who trust in the God who is God. Everyone must, as we have indicated, seek to understand himself, but, to know what one's faith is conceptually, one must have an adequate conceptual way of expressing his faith.

Another problem must be mentioned here, although it cannot be discussed in detail; simply having an adequate conceptuality available as part of one's mental stock does not mean that it will be utilized to express what is actually one's faith. This problem should be clear from the earlier discussions of faith, symbols, and self-understanding. There are psychosociological barriers that interfere with one's knowing what his own faith really is. Part of the task of the theological-educational ministry will be to facilitate the recognition and overcoming of these barriers to self-understanding. At present, in our seminaries, pastoral counseling and certain aspects of Christian education are concerned with these barriers, but a closer correlation of these efforts would seem highly desirable. Indeed, it is impossible to deal adequately with the communications problems relating to the gospel without attempting to understand these barriers.

Christian education practiced as outlined above becomes the testing agent for theology and a bridge between the laity and the theologian. As we have indicated, theology cannot be understood any longer as proceeding from the top down because it is simply not a matter of " saving facts " with which we have to deal. Nor can it be assumed that the Spirit speaks only to scholars about theological matters, or only in Biblical language. It is time for the layman who has come of age to participate in the creation of theology. Theology must be created in dialogue with God's people. In its in-between position, Christian education has a threefold task to perform: teaching, participating in the creating of theology, and serving as the agent of feedback to exegesis and systematics.

It seems proper and necessary that the theological seminaries take the lead in developing what is here called a theological-educational ministry. If such a ministry is to exist, it is clear that the kind of training given in the seminaries will have to reflect the orientation suggested above with respect to theology, Christian education, and the professional ministry. This new ministry demands new kinds of skills and personal qualifications in the minister which most seminaries do not seem able to give. One of the most important of these is the ability to relate appropriately to people. Such an ability requires freedom from defensiveness and the rather deep understanding of oneself and one's limitations that is usually described as humility, and includes a profound interest in others. Ultimately, these are religious qualities. One cannot accept himself and his neighbor in love until he has become willing to receive the forgiveness and love of God. The seminaries will need to become centers for the manifestation of the love of God to the world and to each other within the community of faith. Such an atmosphere will in no way sacrifice scholarly endeavor and honesty, but neither will it equate academic quality with the number of pages read, papers written, or books published. It should be clear that the seminary community must not be secluded from the world, but immersed in it and its life. If as a professional minister one is to serve the laity in order that they may serve the world, he must first learn what it means to serve the world. Such service must be a very important part of seminary life, and it seldom is.

Secondly, such a new kind of ministry must be adequately prepared to be a teaching ministry. This preparation first of all means adequate competence in the basic tradition of the church: the Bible, church history, historical and contemporary theology. In addition, however, there should be adequate preparation for carrying out the process of teaching so that one can avoid wasting the time of all concerned and assure maximum understanding. Skill in this kind of theological education, which has been described as facilitating the communication process that attempts to make Christian faith understandable, is nothing less than skill in helping others work out their theological understanding, their self-understanding before God. For this reason, Christian education as we have described it will be an important part of the preparation for such a ministry. It is vital that one avoid manipulating others or allowing them to be manipulated in a group situation, whether it is accidentally or not. The task is to help the individual or the group to attain an adequate theological conceptuality and in so doing to allow the various voices to be heard and evaluated by the Spirit.

If theology is to be an endeavor of the whole church, if hermeneutics is to be a circle, then some formal means of maintaining the circle will be needed. The first thing that must happen is to eliminate the moratorium on theological debate which has stifled such discussion in the official bodies of most denominations for the past thirty years. The revival of theological debate may mean that we shall have to reopen and complete the unfinished and tragic battle between fundamentalism and liberalism. This particular theological dispute was never resolved because the churches determined to maintain administrative unity instead of theological integrity. Denominational assemblies at the various levels, e.g., presbyteries, conferences, synods, etc. (which, it is presumed, include laity, professional ministry, and seminary faculty), will do what many of them once did, carry on continuous theological discussion and debate as their major business instead of operating as a kind of combination legislative body and sales convention. Such groups will designate areas for study between sessions and arrange for formal debate with which to explore issues and conceptual possibilities. Any theological debate of this seriousness will require an atmosphere free from fear of reprisal for heterodoxy. Honest and profound debate cannot take place where heresy trials are common or where administrative shutout faces those who voice views that sound radical or even possibly heretical to the majority. The limits will have to be broad and this can be countenanced only if the debate is sharp, accurate, and penetrating. The object should be to find the appropriate theological conceptuality by wisdom and prayer, not by authority or majority.

The laity have an important part to play in any such proceedings. It is untenable that they shall be treated as spectators, allowed to listen in on the experts. A laity that has been encouraged and helped to participate in theological thinking by such a theological-educational ministry as has been described above will have a genuine and vital contribution to make in discovering an appropriate theological conceptuality. More than most of the professional ministry, the laity will be free from administrative pressure to conform, either consciously or unconsciously. Further, it is they who are to be the major ministry of the church to the world today and thus can keep the church's debates from being wholly divorced from the real world in which we live.

Local church boards too will need to see part of their major purpose to be theological discussion. Local church boards today are too often occupied totally with budgetary and program matters. But any local church that sees its purpose as understanding and proclaiming the gospel by word and deed will be aware that administration is not the only purpose for any group assembled within the church. One of the best places for the present professional ministry to begin this project of theological education with the laity is within the existing groups of the local church. Let each of them in its own way become a study group.

However, the work of the professional ministry for the laity is hardly begun with the change of these existing groups in the church. The entire mind-set of the church today is in need of revolutionary change. The American church is success-minded and measures its success with the material standards of membership, budget, buildings, church attendance. These must be so devalued as to become meaningless before the church can go about its proper business of manifesting the love of God for the world in its own love for the world. The laity must be helped to view the church building, the worship services, the sacraments, and study groups as beginnings and means, never as ends in themselves.

It is entirely possible that the church of the future will not have at all the form that it presently has with its major manifestation in local congregations. The most important part of the life of the church of the future as a gathered group may be in small groups of varying kinds. For all such groups, the lay academy can be of considerable value by its knowledge of group procedures. More yet, academies can be of great value to professional groups that may well cut across denominational lines. Here one can foresee a group of doctors, or biologists, or atomic scientists, or merchants coming together with the help of professional theologians, educators, and psychologists to discuss their role as Christians in their profession. There is, of course, no reason why such groups cannot or should not form from within the present members of a local church and utilize the services of the present professional ministry. Other kinds of groups are needed too for specialized study or planning. There is a need for parents and educators to meet as Christians to work out some of the educational problems that face us in a pluralistic society. Real estate men and city planners could benefit from such a group situation in considering the effects of their work in a Christian perspective.

Small groups of all kinds could abound in the local church, some utilizing the services of the professional ministry and some not, and their purpose will be to discover ways of expressing God's love to the world in everyday life and how to share that love with one another in community. The professional minister, to be helpful to these groups, will have to minister to them in that most important area of their vocation. Franklin Littell suggests a new kind of specialization for a professional minister, to be a chaplain to a particular vocational community. He is certainly correct in saying there is "no reason why the seminarian should not begin—while still in the B.D. curriculum—to read the magazines, participate in the interdisciplinary seminars and conferences, attend the lay professional conferences, which will make him a capable chaplain to at least one section of the laity in their on-the-job witness."[99]

If denominational assemblies and boards begin to take seriously their position in the hermeneutical circle, many of them will find it useful to employ full-time exegetes, systematic theologians, and Christian educators for the express purpose of assisting the assembly in carrying out the theological task. Such persons might well be employed mainly on a consulting basis and have their major identity with a university or seminary. This latter procedure has much to commend it, for it will make it less necessary for such personnel to follow any denominational party line that might exist. It will be absolutely necessary for those who serve in this capacity to have the equivalent of academic freedom so that they can write, speak, and teach their best convictions without being threatened by denominational hierarchy.

Another way in which the seminaries can enter into this program, and should, is in providing continuing education for the professional ministry. The qualifications, and especially the skills, that have been so briefly outlined above as necessary for the theological-educational ministry have often not been developed by ministers who are now at work. Further, no one can feel that his education is complete when his seminary days are over, or ever, for that matter. A program of continuing education will, first of all, help ministers now at work to gain new knowledge, skills, and qualities and, in some cases, reintroduce them to the church's theological conversation. Secondly, continuing education will be an important way of facilitating interdenominational theological discussion. Thirdly, and perhaps most importantly, it will keep the seminary faculty and the professional ministry in close and continued contact with each other so that understanding can move in both directions.

The whole body of the church includes all the branches of theology, and the whole body is called to the task of understanding its own faith in God. When any one branch of theology or a local congregation claims an inordinate proportion of the total task, the body is ill, not whole. The hermeneutical process is best understood as a circle, not as a one-way arc. If the circle is broken because there is inadequate or ineffective feedback from the general body of believers, or lack of dialogue with them, theology becomes ineffective in its task of facilitating the understanding and expression of faith. Christian education has a vital part to play in the hermeneutical circle to keep it complete, whole. If Christian education does not, or is not allowed to, fulfill its proper part, the hermeneutical circle will be merely an arc and the body of Christ will be ill.

The new image of the ministry as *primarily* theological-educational, rather than primarily preaching or sacramental, puts into practice the understanding that theology is born in interaction within the circle of faith, not spoken in an authoritarian way by the hierarchy.

Heidegger has suggested that every great poet has only one poem and that all his poems are but partial expressions of that one poem. So it is with every specific proclamation of the gospel; it is but *one* of the poems expressing the one poem. The one poem, the one gospel, is never spoken and never can be; man can only speak poems, gospels, the gospel according to . . . Matthew, Mark, Luke, John, Luther, Calvin, Barth, Tillich, you, me. Faith is continually seeking to understand itself. To do so, it composes poems, i.e., tries to express itself in a conceptual way. Worship, study, life itself, may be understood as the recitation of the poems that have been composed. Christian education and the theological-educational ministry in the roles suggested here will be concerned to facilitate the creation of these poems and to evaluate their effectiveness as means of understanding and expressing the one poem.

Notes

1. Cf., e.g., Peter Berger, *The Noise of Solemn Assemblies* (Doubleday & Company, Inc., 1961); Will Herberg, *Protestant —Catholic—Jew: An Essay in American Religious Sociology* (Alfred A. Knopf, Inc., 1951); or Gibson Winter, *The Suburban Captivity of the Churches* (A Macmillan Paperback, 1962).

2. Daniel T. Jenkins, *Beyond Religion* (The Westminster Press, 1962), p. 107.

3. *Ibid.*, p. 108.

4. *Ibid.*, p. 110.

5. *Ibid.*, pp. 110–111.

6. *Ibid.*, p. 113.

7. John A. T. Robinson, *Honest to God* (The Westminster Press, 1963).

8. *Ibid.*, pp. 7–8.

9. *Ibid.*, p. 12.

10. *Ibid.*, pp. 15–16.

11. *Ibid.*, pp. 16–17.

12. John Fry, *The Immobilized Christian* (The Westminster Press, 1963), p. 9.

13. *Ibid.*, p. 23.

14. *Ibid.*, p. 26.

15. In *Religion and Culture: Essays in Honor of Paul Tillich*, ed. by Walter Leibrecht (Harper & Row, Publishers, Inc., 1959), pp. 103–106.

16. Henry P. Van Dusen, *The Vindication of Liberal Theology* (Charles Scribner's Sons, 1963), p. 27.

17. James D. Smart, *The Teaching Ministry of the Church* (The Westminster Press, 1954), pp. 12 f.

18. Cf. Hendrik Kraemer, *A Theology of the Laity* (The Westminster Press, 1959), pp. 64–68.

19. Howard Grimes, *The Rebirth of the Laity* (Abingdon Press, 1962), pp. 53 f.

20. James D. Smart, *op. cit.* p. 50.

21. Horace Bushnell, *Christian Nurture* (Charles Scribner's Sons, 1861), p. 17.

22. *Ibid.*, p. 76.

23. *Ibid.*, pp. 51, 236, 239.

24. *Ibid.*, pp. 90–122.

25. James D. Smart, *op. cit.*, pp. 56 f.

26. H. Richard Niebuhr, Daniel D. Williams, eds., *The Ministry in Historical Perspective* (Harper & Row, Publishers, Inc., 1956), p. 211.

27. *Ibid.*, p. 246.

28. Henry Ward Beecher, *Yale Lectures on Preaching* (J. B. Ford & Co., 1892), p. 88.

29. Niebuhr and Williams, eds., *op. cit.*, p. 259.

30. George A. Coe, *What Is Christian Education?* (Charles Scribner's Sons, 1929).

31. William Clayton Bower, *The Educational Task of the Local Church* (Front Rank Press, 1921).

32. Karl Barth, *Church Dogmatics,* Vol. II, Part 2 (T. & T. Clark, Edinburgh, 1957–1958), p. 3.

33. John Baillie, "Why I Believe in God," *Union Seminary Quarterly Review* (March, 1949).

34. Carlysle Marney, *Faith in Conflict* (Abingdon Press, 1957), p. 35.

35. Harrison Elliott, *Can Religious Education Be Christian?* (The Macmillan Company, 1940), p. 226.

36. Randolph Crump Miller, *The Clue to Christian Education* (Charles Scribner's Sons, 1950), p. vii.

37. James D. Smart, *op. cit.*, p. 65.

38. Randolph Crump Miller, *op. cit.*, p. 11.

39. *Ibid.*, p. 19.

40. *Ibid.*, p. 18.

41. William Hamilton, *The New Essence of Christianity* (Association Press, 1961), p. 29.

42. In *Religious Drama 3: An Anthology of Modern Morality*

Plays, Sel. and Intro. by Marvin Halverson (Meridian Books, 1959), p. 115.

43. *Ibid.*

44. George Herbert Mead, *Mind, Self, and Society* (The University of Chicago Press, 1934).

45. Ernest Hemingway, *A Farewell to Arms* (Charles Scribner's Sons, 1929).

46. Count Leo Tolstoy, *Anna Karenina* (Modern Library, Inc., 1950, originally published 1875).

47. Cf. H. Richard Niebuhr, *Radical Monotheism and Western Civilization* (Harper & Row, Publishers, Inc., 1960), p. 8. I am also greatly indebted to Niebuhr's suggestions for understanding "God and the gods," presented in the essay under that same title in this book.

48. H. Richard Niebuhr, *Radical Monotheism,* p. 118.

49. *Ibid.,* p. 124.

50. Karl Barth, *The Faith of the Church* (Meridian Books, Inc., 1958), p. 48.

51. "The Catechism of the Church of Geneva of (1545)," Questions 28 and 29, in *Calvin: Theological Treatises,* Vol. 22, The Library of Christian Classics (The Westminster Press, 1954), p. 94.

52. Paul Tillich, *The Courage to Be* (Yale University Press, 1952), pp. 180–190.

53. H. Richard Niebuhr, *Radical Monotheism,* pp. 122 f.

54. Rudolf Bultmann, "The Crisis in Belief," in *Essays Philosophical and Theological* (SCM Press, Ltd., 1955), p. 5. (This essay first appeared in German in 1931.)

55. Karl Barth, *The Word of God and the Word of Man* (Harper & Row, Publishers, Inc., 1957), p. 70. (This was first published in German in 1927.)

56. Karl Barth, *The Epistle to the Romans,* 6th ed. (Oxford University Press, 1933), p. 256.

57. *Ibid.*

58. Tillich, *op. cit.,* p. 188.

59. Barth, *The Epistle to the Romans,* p. 225.

60. Cf. Hans W. Bartsch, ed., *Kerygma and Myth* (Harper Torchbook, 1961), which contains the Bultmann essay and others discussing this problem.

61. For a more detailed treatment, cf. Sigmund Mowinckel,

He That Cometh (Abingdon Press, 1954). (The original was published in Danish in 1951.)

62. *Ibid.*, p. 7.

63. *Ibid.*, p. 68.

64. *Ibid.*, p. 71.

65. *Ibid.*

66. *Ibid.*, p. 98.

67. J. Klausner, *Die Messianischen Vorstellung des Jüdischen Volkes im Zeitalter der Tannaiten* (Cracow, 1903), p. 19.

68. Mowinckel, *op. cit.*, pp. 156 f.

69. John Priest, *The Two Messiahs at Qumran* (unpublished Ph.D. dissertation, Drew Theological Seminary, 1960), pp. 77 ff.

70. Mowinckel, *op. cit.*, p. 228.

71. *Ibid.*, pp. 227 f.

72. Aage Bentzen, *King and Messiah* (Lutterworth Press, 1955), p. 71.

73. Rudolf Bultmann, *Primitive Christianity* (Meridian Books, 1957), p. 82.

74. Cf. Bultmann, *Primitive Christianity*, pp. 83 ff.; Bentzen, *op. cit.*, pp. 73–80; Mowinckel, *op. cit.*, pp. 261–279.

75. Bultmann, *Primitive Christianity*, p. 86.

76. Admittedly this is a much disputed point, but recent evidence favors it. Cf. G. H. Boobyer, "Galilee and Galileans in St. Mark's Gospel," *Bulletin of the John Rylands Library*, Vol. 35, No. 2 (March, 1953); Austin Farrer, *St. Matthew and St. Mark* (The Dacre Press, London, 1954); R. H. Lightfoot, *Locality and Doctrine in the Gospels* (Oxford University Press, 1938).

77. Karl Barth, *Der Römerbrief*, pp. 72 ff. English translation quoted from Schubert Ogden, *Christ Without Myth* (Harper & Row, Publishers, Inc., 1961), p. 10.

78. Paul Tillich, *Systematic Theology*, Vol. II (The University of Chicago Press, 1957), p. 126.

79. John Knox, "Christ the Lord," in *Jesus: Lord and Christ* (Harper & Brothers, 1958).

80. Barth, *Der Römerbrief*, p. 72.

81. Ogden, *op. cit.*, pp. 154 f.

82. *Ibid.*

83. Tillich, *Systematic Theology*, p. 115.

84. A difficulty arises as soon as the word "experience" is used because it may refer either to bare phenomenal experi-

ence, i.e., experience *not* cognitively interpreted or to experience as cognitively interpreted. In the sentence at hand, the
phrase "actual experience" refers to the former meaning. In
the usual course of life we do not separate these two aspects
of experience, and perhaps can do so only cognitively, but it is
essential that we recognize that man not only lives in a world
of experience, but that, to a large degree, that world is his own
creation by way of cognitive interpretation. Man thinks or
"thinks up" the world of experience in which he lives to a
surprising degree.

85. The term "history" is here used to refer to any recording
or recounting of past events. History is necessarily cognitively
interpreted experience because it is captured in cognitive symbols, i.e., language.

86. Religion as used here will refer to that which is a matter
of faith; and faith will mean the organizing principle, or cen-
tralizing factor of human personality. This definition is intended to encompass both Tillich's "ultimate concern" and
H. Richard Niebuhr's duality of trust and loyalty. Further, it
emphasizes the necessity of including cognition, will, and emotion in discussing any religious meaning of history.

87. Experience is used at this point to mean "experience as
cognitively interpreted"; this is the usual everyday usage of
the word.

88. Cf. Gilbert Ryle, *Dilemmas* (Cambridge University
Press, 1960), pp. 93–111.

89. For any of the past to be meaningful in any serious sense
it must tell us something about the present. The fact, for example, that Rome was not built in a day is not meaningful
apart from what it says about large tasks to be undertaken
now. If Pompeii is a dead volcano in fact, then the fact that
it once exploded tells us nothing about living beside dead
volcanoes, only about potentially live ones.

90. Cf. Friedrich Gogarten, *Demythologizing and History*,
tr. by Neville Horton (Charles Scribner's Sons, 1955), pp. 37–38.

91. Karl Jaspers, *The Perennial Scope of Philosophy* (Rout-
ledge & Kegan Paul, Ltd., London, 1950), p. 46.

92. *Ibid.*, p. 48.

93. Rudolf Bultmann, *Faith and Existence* (Living Age
Books, 1960), p. 46.

94. Religious meaning is the answer to the questions: What

is life all about? What for and why do we live? Is life more
than a mad molecular dance to death? It is that kind of question
which concerned the Biblical writers, and they see its answer in
the appropriate state of relationships between God, man, and
neighbor.

95. Rudolf Bultmann, *Essays Philosophical and Theological,*
p. 251.

96. *Ibid.*

97. Cf. Gogarten, *op. cit.*, pp. 70–75.

98. W. H. Auden, "For the Time Being," in *The Collected
Poetry of W. H. Auden* (Random House, Inc., 1945), p. 454.

99. Franklin H. Littell, "The Apostolate of the Laity and
Theological Education," in *The Inter Seminarian,* Vol. 2, No. 1
(May, 1963), p. 3.